PARADIGM FOUND

PARADIGM FOUND

LEADING AND MANAGING FOR
POSITIVE CHANGE

Anne Firth Murray

New World Library
Novato, California

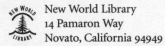 New World Library
14 Pamaron Way
Novato, California 94949

Copyright © 2006 by Anne Firth Murray

Text design and typography by Tona Pearce Myers

Library of Congress Cataloging-in-Publication Data
Murray, Anne Firth.
Paradigm found : leading and managing for positive change / Anne Firth Murray.
    p.   cm.
Includes bibliographical references and index.
ISBN-13: 978-1-57731-533-9 (pbk. : alk. paper)
1. Nonprofit organizations—Management. 2. Non-governmental organizations—Management. 3. Social action. 4. Corporate culture. 5. Women in development—Case studies. 6. Global Fund for Women. 7. Murray, Anne Firth. I. Title.
HD62.6.M87 2006
658—dc22   2006001298

First printing, May 2006
ISBN-10: 1-57731-533-2
ISBN-13: 978-1-57731-533-9
Printed in Canada on partially recycled, acid-free paper

g   A proud member of the Green Press Initiative

Distributed by Publishers Group West

10   9   8   7   6   5   4   3   2   1

To the women and gentle men
who dare to follow principles
for positive change.

If the cause is right, the means will come.

— Gandhi

Contents

Foreword

My life path as a donor activist dates from a lunch with Anne
Firth Murray on a sunny June day in 1987. Over sandwiches at
a sidewalk café in downtown Palo Alto, California, Anne told
me about her vision for The Global Fund for Women and invited me to join the group of founding donors. As she talked, I
found myself becoming more and more excited about this fledg-
ling idea. By the time our coffee had arrived, I was ready to write
a check on the spot — the very first time I had ever done anything like that. Looking back now after eighteen years, I ask myself, Why?

I had known Anne as the population program officer at the
Hewlett Foundation for several years, and we had also been part
of occasional gatherings to discuss international women's issues.
I already had a great deal of respect for Anne's intelligence, her
passion, and her commitment to making the world a better
place. But what captured me immediately about her vision for

this new organization were two things: *what* she wanted to do and *how* she proposed to do it.

One need only look at the context of the times during the early days of The Fund to see that the *what* — The Fund's focus on global women's rights — was radical and unusual. This was well before the 1994 Cairo International Conference on Population and Development, when philanthropists and activists established a clear link between population issues and improving the status of women. Before Cairo, donors could claim (and many did) that population programs were high on their agendas, but practically in the same breath they would declare, "We don't fund women's issues." Thus Anne's focus on women made sense for practical reasons: improving the situation of women is a tremendously effective leverage point for addressing many of the world's problems. There are compelling social justice reasons as well: we cannot in good conscience stand by while the human rights of half the world's people may be compromised simply because of their gender.

However, in Anne's vision, the *how* was even more important than the *what*, and it was certainly just as radical for the times. Anne believed that the true experts were the women the organization wished to serve and that the best way to be effective was to listen to those women. They would tell us what the problems were and how they could best address them, and we would put resources directly into their hands. On the part of the grantees, there would be no translation necessary, both literally and figuratively. They could submit their proposals in any language, and The Global Fund would find a volunteer to translate. The directness of this model ensured that nothing would be lost in translation between a well-intentioned funder and the grassroots groups that were actually doing the work. Anne envisioned Global Fund grantees as partners sharing power and trust.

With The Global Fund for Women, Anne pioneered a new ethos of philanthropy, creating an organization that would truly involve the people it hoped to serve. As we have seen from the success of Global Fund grantees around the world, the effects of this style of philanthropy are transformative.

During my eight years on The Global Fund's board I met grantees from every continent — incredible women who indeed have proven to be the experts in knowing the needs of their communities and how best to address them. In 1991, shortly after joining the board, I traveled to Bangladesh and Nepal. I met women like Rita Thapa of Kathmandu, who became a Global Fund grantee and later a board member and who has since founded two organizations in Nepal: Tewa, the Nepal Women's Fund, inspired by the model of The Global Fund for Women; and Nagarik Aawaz, a Nepali peace-building organization.

There are many of us around the world who, like Rita Thapa, have been personally influenced by the principles and the model that Anne describes in this book. Maya Ajmera, president and founder of the Global Fund for Children, first came across Anne's work when she was a young graduate student. Mesmerized by the model of small grants to women's human rights organizations, she thought, If we can do it with women, we can do it with children. Indigenous-led organizations, such as those the Global Fund for Children supports, are powerful, and they are sustainable. By giving small grants locally, one can do great things in the developing world, as the work of The Global Fund for Women and now also the Global Fund for Children has demonstrated.

Jennifer Astone, executive director of the Firelight Foundation, is a former staff member of The Global Fund for Women. Shortly after Jen joined The Global Fund, Anne (who had already retired as president) gave a series of tea talks for the staff. Jen recalls that Anne told "the most riveting story" about The Global Fund, how it had all started, and what she had done to implement her vision. Anne's ideas about funding at the local level and working in partnership with grassroots women meshed with Jen's own view of development. Jen was inspired by Anne, who had taken on the roots of change in philanthropy, bucked the system, and labored for years to realize her vision. In her work with the Firelight Foundation, whose mission is to support children orphaned or affected by HIV/AIDS in Sub-Saharan Africa, Jen continues to champion the model of making small grassroots grants overseas. She considers Firelight a sister organization of The Global Fund in terms of advancing this model.

The idea for Youth Philanthropy Worldwide (YPW), an organization that I cofounded, originated at a Take Our Daughters to Work Day at The Global Fund for Women. That day, a lively group of middle-school girls discussed Global Fund grants. Seeking to build the next generation of global citizens who would support powerful and effective social change organizations, we at YPW looked first to The Global Fund for a stellar model of such an organization. As YPW's work has evolved, Anne's principles remain a guide: listen to the people you serve; we are both givers and receivers in the global community; and people on the ground know best what the problems are and how to address them.

These are but a few examples among many of Anne's far-reaching influence. I hope there will be even more, as readers of this book find inspiration in its practical suggestions and clear guidelines for thinking about their own philanthropic work in new ways.

The Global Fund for Women is flourishing today. The strength of Anne's original vision is reflected not only in all those whose work she has influenced but also in the continuing success of the organization. The Fund has given away millions of dollars to thousands of women's organizations in every corner of the globe. For me, The Global Fund is the gold standard for international women's rights organizations, and Anne's story is well worth reading. To this day, Anne is an inspiration to me, and my contribution as a founding donor to The Global Fund for Women remains the best five thousand dollars I have ever spent.

— Esther B. Hewlett

Prologue

[She] has achieved success who has lived well, laughed often and loved much; who has gained the respect of intelligent [people] and the love of little children; who has filled [her] niche and accomplished [her] task; who has left the world better than [she] found it, whether by an improved poppy, a perfect poem or a rescued soul; who has never lacked appreciation of Earth's beauty or failed to express it; who has always looked for the best in others and given them the best [she] had; whose life was an inspiration; whose memory a benediction.

— Bessie Stanley

We all strive to succeed in life, and for many of us, personal success is directly related to our contributions to the world around us. We dream and hope for a better world, and we find meaning in our lives by following our dreams and trying to turn them into reality. This book is for people who want to succeed in making the world a better place and who want to be inspired by specific evidence that positive change is possible.

A couple of decades ago, I challenged myself to figure out my own mission and goals. After some focused time and heartfelt searching, I determined that I had two primary goals: to feel at peace with myself and to make a positive difference in the world. I am still working to attain these goals, which I find to be basically interconnected. Over the years, working in the world of international development, I have found meaning by building organizations and environments that have made a difference to many people.

One organization in particular has caught the imagination of many people around the world. It is The Global Fund for Women, which I cofounded in 1987 and built into a worldwide funding network supporting women globally. In this book, we explore why and how the vision, principles, and practice of this particular nongovernmental and philanthropic organization came to mean so much to so many people. The success of The Global Fund for Women, which is the largest nonprofit organization focusing specifically on women's rights in the world, suggests that developing new paradigms for interaction may be both effective and necessary if we are to make the world a more positive place.

Looking back almost ten years after retiring from The Global Fund, I realize that I learned some valuable lessons as founding president. The organization has not only survived but thrived. Many people have asked me how I grew The Fund from the seed of an idea into a mature, living organization. What were the early steps that we took to make it work? Can we learn by looking back?

From the beginning at The Global Fund for Women we had a dream of a better world for both women and men. This dream was shared by many people and articulated in the first annual report of The Fund: we sought to enhance the social, economic, and political position of women worldwide in order to "weave together women's experience, wisdom, and power to achieve justice and dignity for all life on earth."[1]

Before the creation of The Fund, I had spent years working on international development issues, and I strongly believed that we needed new ways of approaching international problems, new players, and new types of institutions to effect positive change. I had a vision of a world in which people of very diverse backgrounds would have the freedom to lead productive and meaningful lives and treat each other with respect, trust, and love. The Global Fund became a vehicle for attempting to make these dreams reality.

From the very beginning, many people were willing to work — and work very hard — to make The Global Fund for Women succeed. I for one was driven to make it happen. For many reasons, mostly having to do with where I was in my life at that time, the idea meshed with my personal experience, needs, goals, and dreams. And I had friends and cofounders who not only provided ideas, support, and criticism but also put in the time and effort needed to get The Fund under way. They located legal help, reviewed materials, and participated in endless sessions spent brainstorming and then refining ideas. Soon many other people became committed to our shared vision and worked very hard to realize it.

The process through which we were going to carry out our vision and goals — giving money to women's groups around the world to result in their empowerment — was something I knew about. I had worked in the world of philanthropy for twenty years, giving away money. I knew how to do grant-making well, with respect and trust, and always with the intent of empowering the grantee.

But there were many things that I did not know how to do — things like fund-raising. So, as we started out, it seemed natural to adopt a learning-and-listening mode; what we didn't know, we would learn from people who did. We had our ears and eyes wide open, working in an entrepreneurial way, and that style continued through the years. In retrospect, we found that we had created a learning organization much like the model that Peter Senge describes in his 1990 book *The Fifth Discipline: The Art and Practice of the Learning Organization*.[2] We had quickly recognized that making connections and striving to be as inclusive as possible helped us *and* The Global Fund.

Most important, we put together a set of guiding principles that allowed us to develop a way of operating that was consistent with our values. I came to believe and often state that without a doubt *the way we did our work was more important than what we did*. I still feel that way today, and I apply this principle in my everyday life, in the classes I teach at Stanford University, and in my interactions with my grandchildren and all others.

⋙⊚⋘⊚⋙

The earliest thinking behind the creation of The Global Fund was very much like a seed — specifically, a tiny raspberry seed stuck in my wisdom tooth. I was overseeing the environmental and population programs at the William and Flora Hewlett Foundation at the time, and I fretted about the state of the world. I worried about how I could make things better, and I bemoaned the fact that very little money was going from U.S. foundations to support women-run organizations internationally.

This was in the early 1980s, when some of us knew how central women were to development but very few donors were focusing specifically on women's leadership and women-governed and women-managed organizations. The idea of creating a new organization developed over time and crystallized during a dinner conversation in 1987 with two women who became cofounders and founding board members of The Global Fund. By early 2006, The Fund had grown into an organization that had provided $47 million in grants to 2,991 women's groups in 162 countries.

We identified and filled an important niche — the need for small, strategic amounts of money for women's groups that had just formed or that were already established but needed a boost to get to the next level of operation. We sought to seed, strengthen, and link women's groups by giving such grants in a timely way.

At the very beginning, this kind of seed money was also needed by The Global Fund itself, and in its first year The Fund received a few personal donations from friends and cofounders; donations of five thousand dollars from people whom we called "founding donors"; a modest grant and an office from the David and Lucile Packard Foundation; as well as a few in-kind gifts, such as an Apple computer and printer and pro bono legal advice.

This early money and help, given with such trust and optimism mostly by family and friends, came at just the right moment. We had a vision and a plan, and we needed money to implement our plan. This is what I wanted The Global Fund to do for other women. I wanted The Global Fund to say and mean, "We believe in you and your dreams, and you are not alone." The money is important, but just as important is the good feeling that comes from having an idea, believing you can move forward, and having someone from the outside support you. I am reminded of one of Thich Nhat Hanh's basic mantras on true love: "Dear One, I am here for you."[3] That is how I wanted The Global Fund to be for women in poorer countries around the world — to be there for them.

From the beginning, The Global Fund for Women put money

into the hands of women so they could change their own societies in their own terms. Women themselves defined their own problems and solutions. Our role was to provide the support to allow their voices to be heard and their choices to be respected. This meant that The Fund supported groups working on a wide range of human rights issues, including ending gender-based violence and building peace, ensuring economic and environmental justice, advancing health care and sexual and reproductive rights, and expanding civic and political participation. At first we focused on groups that were either too small or too ahead of their time to be supported by other sources. We especially responded to groups whose approach attempted to transform the way women were perceived or the way they perceived themselves in their societies. Later we supported larger groups, networks, conferences, and other mechanisms designed by women to strengthen women.

We envisioned a world changed in positive ways, a world where women would be fully empowered. We raised money to give it away, and we did this in such a way that we hoped to blur the lines between givers and receivers. We saw all as activists, all as donors, all as givers and receivers. Always we provided "general support," flexible money that nurtured freedom and creativity.

As we began to define and state our guiding principles clearly, I tried to lead and manage the young organization in a style that allowed the staff, board members, grantees, and donors to interact as respected equals. It was and is my belief that if we are to survive as human beings we must treat each other in an evenhanded way. When I accepted the Council on Foundations' Robert W. Scrivner Award for Creative Grantmaking, in April 1996, I made this simple, familiar, and heartfelt statement of belief: "If we are to change the world for the better, we must treat one another as we

ourselves wish to be treated." The personal is political, and I
wanted this new organization to exemplify these ideas.

Throughout the first decade of The Global Fund for Women,
I met many people, both men and women, who were moved by
what we were trying to do. Of course, the women's groups that
we supported were excited to be linked to a new funding agency.
But The Fund was not just a source of money; it served as a
means of connecting with others and creating community both
within the United States and around the world. There was something about what we did — and more important, about the way
we did it — that struck a chord. The Fund ultimately added
meaning to the lives of thousands of women and men — women
in small organizations around the world, advisors, donors, volunteers, staff people, and board members.

☜☜☜☜☜

An important reason for writing this book is simply that many
people have asked me to do it. They have urged me to describe
what I have learned in my years in the nonprofit and international world, particularly as founding president of The Global
Fund for Women. Many of the people who have urged me to do
this are women working in poorer countries around the world.
They want to know how it is possible to start from scratch, with
an idea based on certain heartfelt — I would say "feminist" —
principles, and end up with an efficient and effective organization. I want to describe in a personal way how we did this on a
day-to-day basis, what we did when principles and values con-
flicted, and how we positioned The Global Fund successfully in a
world that does not always value such consistency of principles.
Furthermore, in my reading of current organizational theory, I

have found very little on the actual application of ideas to a real organization. I have found little that describes the nuts and bolts of putting principles into practice. This is another reason for sharing my real-world experiences.

My hope, therefore, is to describe our "paradigm found," a way of doing business that may not be entirely new but appears to have been hidden or perhaps lost. It is a way of being that seems to belong to less harsh, less violent, more graceful, and more loving times, and it needs to be rediscovered, if it ever truly existed. Let's hope that such times await us in the future.

This book recounts a process that others have attempted to describe — the development of an organization from its beginning through the transition from its founding leadership. Although many people would argue that this unfolding is very similar from one organization to another, we know that the world of organizations is like the world itself — a place of great diversity, challenge, and surprise. Some explorers in this world have a mechanistic bent and therefore describe what they experience and observe in such terms, laying out blueprints and rules to be followed by those who are in positions of control and direction. Others see the world of organizations more organically, as a kind of natural world in which there is order as well as seeming chaos, in which opportunities and surprises may be more relevant than notions of "the way things should be." My approach falls into the second category; I feel most comfortable conceiving of an organization as an environment in which surprising and beautiful things can happen and grow, much like a garden.

We will discuss metaphors for organizations elsewhere in this book, but often the idea of wandering through a garden will surface, as we describe the beginnings of things — the seeds and seedlings, if you will — and the growth of the organization with the help of wise advisors, workers, and friends. We will speak about what it takes to maintain a healthy organizational environment, whether that involves plenty of water (i.e., commitment and passion), fertilizer (i.e., money), or open space (i.e., freedom). We will discuss how one learns from one's actions, what can be done when the organization grows almost too quickly, how one can manage stressful change, and so on. Although the order of such discussions may not be entirely obvious, it seems logical to start at the beginning, with the vision and the early steps, and move in roughly chronological order through discussions of principles and actions, including the eventual retirement of the first gardener.

The growth of the organization, from its beginning to its fullness, is represented in the cover and text images of *koru*, which in the Maori language of New Zealand symbolizes not only the unfolding of the fern frond striving toward the light, but also a new beginning, renewal, and hope for the future.

In creating a garden — even a rather wild and informal one, which is the kind that I prefer — one can plant too many things, overwater, or make the mistake of introducing some plants that may not fit in or grow well with others. One must consciously and continuously try to strike a balance in which every plant gets the space, the nutrients, and the care it needs. The creation of an organization can be as delightful as creating a lovely garden or as sad as seeing plants that one has cared for wither and die. So much depends on vision, hard work, cultivation, and balance.

In the pages that follow, I chronicle some of what happened, but more than that I try to share what I have learned, not just in the creation of The Global Fund but also in the period that preceded and followed that creation. One evening I was talking with two other women about the need for an organization that would make money available to women around the world to change their societies in ways that they defined, and the next day I was determined — I was fanatically driven, really — to make this happen, to raise millions of dollars, and to change the world through the empowerment of women. This passion galvanized and sustained me through the beginnings and the growth of The Global Fund, through the difficulties of actually raising the money and developing the systems that served The Fund so well over the years, and through the problems I faced when I tried to stick to principles and my intentions were misunderstood.

⋘◎≼◎◎≽◎≽⋙

Why should we look to new paradigms of organizational development? We do this because so many organizations seem woefully inadequate to respond to the needs of our current world, which is rapidly changing. Some say that we are drifting inevitably toward anarchy and disorder. Violence and loss have become more and more commonplace, as unthinkable events, such as 9/11, the Columbine killings, mass rapes, the New Orleans flood debacle, the tsunami and the earthquakes in Asia, and the slaughter of thousands in Rwanda and Sudan, flash across our global consciousness. Again and again, so-called leaders emerge who rely on dominance, violence, elitism, misrepresentation, racism, and sexism to wield power.

At the same time, there is an almost desperate hunger for some understanding of what the future will hold. Are we losing control? Why is violence proliferating? How can we find meaning and community in our lives in the face of such rapid change? Politicians are voted in and out of office as people cast about for help in understanding their changing circumstances. People's hunger to find meaning in their lives is fueled by the fear and violence that characterize our time.

Vaclav Havel, the former president of the Czech Republic, has said that the "modern age has ended.... We are going through a transitional period, when it seems that something is on the way out and something else is painfully being born. It is as if something were crumbling, decaying, and exhausting itself, while something else, still indistinct, were arising from the rubble."[4]

Have I been shaken by events? Yes. Do I despair? Sometimes. But because of my experiences over the past decades in developing new ways of organizing and working and especially learning from women's groups around the world, I have hope. I see new patterns and models of human interaction emerging globally, models that are created from the good in people. This book is about the "something else, still indistinct," which is arising amid violence and chaos. It is also about ways that women in particular are dealing with the disintegration of assumptions about the world. Drawing on the experiences of women, the poorest of the poor worldwide, we can learn a great deal. Personally and in community, women and gentle men are creating organizations and systems — new or rediscovered paradigms — characterized by compassion, diversity, generosity, inclusiveness, respect, and shared learning.

As part of my classes on international women's health issues, I encourage my students to email me weekly with their thoughts and reactions to whatever we are studying. In one such response, a twenty-year-old student wrote, "I am struck by how much wrong there is in the world, how much further we as women and as believers in equality have to go. The description of [India, in the class readings] was so difficult to reconcile with the view from my bedroom window, of a street and park at Stanford that represents so much comfort and luxury.... It's so heartening to know that there are women all over the world who will stop at nothing to achieve what they believe they deserve. I can't imagine how difficult it must be for them, but I am so glad to see their strength and resolve, because I hope that somewhere I have even a fraction of that within myself."

I responded to this student by saying that when I began to develop The Global Fund for Women and learned over time how many women and other very poor people were forcefully and actively making positive change, I was able to be hopeful. Now, many years later and in the face of destruction, deprivation, and despair in many parts of the world, I learn from the students — and my hope continues to grow. It is exciting and reassuring to realize that we are not alone in our desire to change the world for the better.

CHAPTER ONE

Believe Positive Change
Is Possible

———— ✺✺✺✺ ————

*Despair over our own powerlessness is simply a lie we keep
telling ourselves.*

— Tony Kushner

Perhaps you have had the feeling while reading a newspaper, listening to a lecture, or sitting around a dinner table talking with
friends about current events, that "Something ought to be done
about that!" Or perhaps you have felt appalled by an injustice or
some sad event and thought, "What is to be done?" Such shock
or sadness about the state of the world signals our recognition
that things can be otherwise.

Living in a world where there is tremendous access to information and communication, more and more people are becoming aware that their lives can be different, that alternatives are

possible, and even that people may have a *right* to better lives. This recognition of a problem and the feeling that there are alternatives to the status quo are the beginnings of change. Believing that change is possible allows a person to dream and develop a vision for change and a plan of action.

Looking Within Ourselves for Answers

Two weeks after September 11, 2001, the day of the destruction and human tragedy at the World Trade Center and the Pentagon in the United States, I attended a panel discussion at Stanford University at which three scholars tried to explain why the attacks had occurred and what it meant in terms of U.S. foreign policy. After the presentations, the audience seemed stunned. I supposed that we were still trying to make sense of what we were feeling and thinking about the attacks.

My own initial shock had subsided, only to be replaced by extreme anxiety about what the U.S. response might be. The attacks brought to my mind so many complicated thoughts — the dangers of extremism, the desperation of people who have been deprived of freedom, the demeaning treatment of women, the misuse of power. Surely other audience members were also wrestling with such thoughts, and this explained their subdued reaction to the panel.

Eventually, a few people in the audience raised some academic questions. And then a young woman rose and cried out, "What can I do? What can we do? You are faculty members. Tell us what we are supposed to do about what has happened!" The room fell silent. The panel members just looked at each other, apparently hoping that someone would think of some answer.

I sat nervously collecting my thoughts and wondering whether

I should say what I was thinking and feeling. This was a distinguished, informed panel, and I was a relatively new member of the faculty. If they didn't have answers, who did? But the young student held my attention. I could feel her anxiety, her intense desire to do something in the wake of this horrific event, her belief that change was possible, and her trust that she would receive wise direction from those in authority.

The situation reminded me of a similar experience that had occurred years earlier in my life. In 1983, I watched a widely broadcast television program called *The Day After*, which depicted possible nuclear destruction.[1] The program was followed immediately by a televised panel discussion of nuclear issues and what could be done about them. The panel, moderated by Ted Koppel, featured a group of experts: William Buckley, Jr., Henry Kissinger, Robert McNamara, Carl Sagan, George Shultz, Brent Scowcroft, and Elie Wiesel. They spoke of the seeming inevitability of nuclear war and some of the things that they had been trying to do to prepare for it, like building up military strength.

As I listened to these experts, I became increasingly alarmed. If they saw nuclear violence as a probable outcome, they would act in those terms. But wouldn't giving reality to the idea of a nuclear war make it all the more possible? If this panel of experts could not imagine peace, I thought to myself, then perhaps peace was not possible? No! I refused to accept this. But I was still full of anxiety because it seemed to me that in the face of the possibility of global destruction, these people were thinking incorrectly. They were thinking of winning the game instead of changing the game, of dominance over others instead of relationship with others. And they were offering no hope of peace, which seemed to me to be outrageous. As far as I could tell, these authorities with power and knowledge were admitting that they had no idea or even a vision of how to prevent such a disaster. Were these the people we should be looking to for answers?

Often, like the young woman at Stanford, we look to established authorities for guidance — and all too often, we are disappointed. Are we at a loss because we are asking the wrong questions? Do we lack imagination? Is a major paradigm shift required for real change to occur?

In the early 1980s, spurred by the growing global distress I was seeing through my work in international development, I read several books that offered interesting perspectives and insights: *The Fate of the Earth*, by Jonathan Schell,[2] dealt with the threat of nuclear war but held out some hope for change; *In a Different Voice*, by Carol Gilligan,[3] explored the different ways that males and females perceive moral dilemmas and offered insights about various ways of thinking; and *The Return of the Goddess*, by Edward Whitmont,[4] stressed the importance of recovering the feminine in each person as a way of achieving balance in a violent world.

I reflected on some of these readings as I watched the panel discussion of *The Day After* on that evening in 1983, and I began to realize that the panelists — all men — did not know what to do! Oddly enough, I felt that I might know what to do — not because I was learned but because I was convinced that there had to be alternative ways to proceed. There had to be answers, I affirmed to myself — and this fundamental belief served as an antidote to despair and, most important, spurred me to action. I felt driven, almost breathless, as I thought of how important and necessary it was to do *something*. I decided at that time to support as many groups working on social justice and women's issues — particularly those addressing violence — as I could. I bought copies of the books that had inspired me and gave them to friends. And I began to feel a stirring to create some network, some organization, based on the idea of reaching out across differences with mutual respect and compassion.

Nearly twenty years later, years after creating The Global Fund for Women but just two weeks after 9/11, I found myself sitting in a meeting room at the Women's Center at Stanford, waiting once again for a panel of respected authorities to provide meaningful answers. Then I stood up and heard myself say, "There *are* things you can do." I spoke directly to the young woman who had cried out in distress. "You can reach out to others and be kind. You can seek out people different from yourself who seem worried and alone and talk with them. You can change how you live your life. You can write to the media. You can write to Congress. Tell them what you think, feel, and believe."

I went on to share my thoughts about how I believe our roles change as we move through life. In the first third of life (to about age thirty), I believe that we must learn skills and clarify our beliefs and values. In the second third (from ages thirty to sixty), we are at the center of our lives, when we can apply what we have learned to make the world a better place. And in the final third (after age sixty), we may move to the edges, still learning and supporting others in their learning and their actions by sharing our experience and our knowledge. I said to the student, "You are in the first third of life. This is your time to learn and acquire skills. Be an excellent student. Learn languages. Clarify and strengthen your values and purpose. Become competent, generous, and kind. Then, in the next third, as you apply your learning in terms of your values, you will be equipped to make a real difference in the world."

When I had finished, the audience stood and applauded,

which surprised me. Everything I had said, it seemed to me, was obvious. But I think I had struck a chord because my words had offered optimism and hope as well as a modest plan of action.

Envisioning Change in a World of Hierarchy

A plan of action is crucial because social change and the righting of wrongs must go beyond the initial recognition of a problem. We need to feel empowered to take the next step — to try to figure out what can be done and whether we ourselves can do it. Perhaps we can take action together with other people, inspiring them or helping them. It is one thing to feel bad about a situation and to feel that something ought to be done about it. It is quite another to believe that something can be done about it and that you yourself can take action to bring about change.

Limiting some of us from moving forward is the way in which we view each other socially. The current paradigm, a hierarchical pattern of relating, leads us to feel separated from one another, leaving some people disempowered and others filled with arrogance. Our societies are based for the most part on the idea that things can be explained in *either/or* and *win/lose* terms, so we constantly judge each person or way of doing things as better or worse than others rather than as just different from them. Such hierarchical thinking has resulted in the idea that some country or some person is "number one" or at the "top." And it can lead to the absolutist view that "you are either with us or against us!" In reality, life is much more complicated than that. In truth, each of us is one among many. The trick is to organize social relationships in such a way that we all gain rather than some losing in order for others to "win." This paradigm shift — moving from *either/or* to *both/and* and from *win/lose* to *win/win* — stems from holding certain views about the world. And not everyone shares those views.

Many people are convinced, for example, that "there will always be poor people." Many people think that violence is inevitable. And many are convinced that command and control organizational forms are natural. As long as we are living in a world where the typical pattern of social relations is such that one group considers itself or is considered better or more important than another (white vs. black, male vs. female, rich vs. poor, educated vs. illiterate, gay vs. straight, young vs. old), many people will feel disempowered and thus impotent to solve the problems that face us.

This hierarchical or patriarchal system of dominance and submission is impractical and wasteful. It does not allow for the valuable contributions of people who have been marginalized, and it shuts off true learning among people who are different from one another. For example, we can now say with some certainty, in the context of terrorism and the rise of fundamentalism in many parts of the world, that regimes and movements that demean women, that are threatened by women's participation and power, and that seek to eliminate the human rights of women truly threaten global existence. So, too, with the destruction of the environment: actions that destroy rather than protect, that exploit rather than nurture, threaten the basic health of the planet.

Paradigm shifts take time. They are painful. When old ways of thinking and behaving begin to move aside for the new, there is a time of grief, even for those people who welcome the new. Grieving is essentially a time of adapting to a new set of assumptions. A loved one dies, and everything changes. We grieve as we rebuild our world around different assumptions. Therefore, if one consciously wants to bring about a paradigm change, one will be working not just for change but also in the context of grief — the grief that comes with loss and major change.

Clearly, old patterns of categorizing people and assigning values to the categories are no longer working. This dichotomizing has separated us from each other, individual from individual and country from country, at the very time when it is most possible to connect with each other and work together toward a more positive future. I am convinced that continuing to structure interpersonal, professional, and international relations on the basis of *either/or*, and *we/they* with one or the other being valued more, leads to domination, violence, and conquest, threatening the survival of the planet and certainly the survival of those being dominated, violated, or conquered. We need to avoid such separation and fragmentation and work toward community and cohesion.

But how can we move to a new paradigm of social relations? We seem to be caught in a web of institutions — medical systems, legal systems, governmental systems, universities — that are based on hierarchy, with positional leadership and a pyramid of underlings subjected to rules from the top. What's more, we have been enamored for too long with bottom-line linear thinking; we often attempt to solve some narrowly defined problem, rather than trying to understand fully the complexities of issues in relationship to other people and then seeking to strengthen those relationships in the interest of discovering peaceful and effective solutions. A few moments spent listening to or reading the daily news suffice to show where current paradigms, which emphasize winning rather than collaborating, fragmenting rather than integrating, have led us.

For example, the world is characterized by violence and poverty. The violence should not surprise us since violence is a strategy used by those in power to maintain the status quo. Violence proliferates at all levels; there are some thirty or forty civil wars raging around the world at the moment. And, on average, one out of every three women in the world will experience violence at the hands of an intimate partner. Poverty also persists; as populations grow, more people rather than fewer are living on one or two dollars a day. Most of the poorest of the poor are women, positioned at the bottom of the hierarchy.

Persistent violence and poverty not only highlight the systems of hierarchy within which we live; they also underscore the fact that current institutions and political structures in the for-profit, government, and even nonprofit worlds are proving perilously inadequate to cope with pluralism and rapid change. The nonprofit sector — often called civil society — is of vital importance here. One promising trend is the dynamic growth of nonprofit and voluntary associations, from consumer movements to grassroots groups to advocacy organizations. Globally, such groups are beginning to mature and gain skills. They are becoming critical to the progress of democracy, especially in regions such as eastern Europe and southern Africa. Most important, new groups and organizations must be created that exemplify new paradigms of interaction based on principles of compassion, trust, transparency, diversity, respect, and other values that will bring people into community rather than divide them.

The primary reason for creating a nongovernmental non-profit organization — often called a civil society organization — is to express an altruistic vision and consciously work toward attaining that vision for positive social change. Civil society organizations are the vehicles for the hopes and dreams of many individual people, for their drive to find meaning in their lives. These organizations provide places where men and women can express their desire for change, their ideals, their commitments, and their compassion. They are places where the heartfelt beliefs of people can find a home, where the precious bases of civil society and democracy can be nurtured, and where democracy itself can find refuge in times of disintegration, deprivation, and despair.

Civil society, which is vibrant and growing in almost every country of the world, consists of thousands of organizations, both large and small, that are designed to serve the common good and to express people's noble ideals. It is within civil society that there is hope for new paradigms of interaction. The three sectors of society — civil society, business, and government — interact and often overlap. A strong civil society sector reduces the possibility that one of the other sectors will dominate society or abuse power; it serves as an important balance to the business and government sectors. Creating strong, well-governed, and well-managed civil society organizations is therefore of great importance for a healthy free society. In the course of my time with The Global Fund for Women, I came to see our work as not just giving funds to women's groups but as working with them to include and strengthen marginalized people in order for them to participate fully in their societies' structures of power and governance.

After violence and poverty, what other seemingly overwhelming forces would lead us to actively seek new paradigms in social relations? There are many. Issues of global warming, toxic contamination, and especially water and fuel shortages, for example, affect all people but especially burden poor women in poor countries as they must walk farther and farther to gather fuel and water, and they must work in fields where they may be exposed to harmful chemicals. Environmental degradation is a major economic, health, and human rights issue for people living in poor countries and for those concerned about them. In response, the worldwide environmental movement, parts of which are based on community, shared learning, and respect for the planet and for humanity, is gaining strength.

Some see the sheer numbers of people on this globe as the key problem at the heart of some of the issues we have mentioned. Global population continues to increase at about 1.4 percent a year, with virtually all of the growth taking place in poorer countries. Although the world population growth rate is declining over time, the actual number of people added to the global population will remain high for several decades. World population is estimated to reach about 9.3 billion (compared with the current 6.5 billion) by the middle of this century, according to the Population Reference Bureau, a Washington-based research organization. The number of people needing housing, jobs, and food is staggering. Slum suburbs have mushroomed in Lagos, Nigeria; Lima, Peru; Mexico City, Mexico; Nairobi, Kenya; and many other urban areas. Governments are unable to build schools or train teachers fast enough to keep up with growing populations of young people. Currently, about 90 percent of all of the world's people are living in poor countries.

In the meantime, modern communications technology spreads like a fire around the globe. It holds both hope and some dangers. This continuing global advancement and expansion of communications and computer technology threatens to leave marginalized people — including women — behind, without influence over the way in which such technology is used and whom it will benefit. Furthermore, widespread media access to information about all parts of the world is a double-edged sword. It brings greater understanding, but it also highlights inequities. People know about all sorts of things that are simply unavailable to them. The challenge is to ensure that access to new technologies includes marginalized people and strengthens civil society as it grows and balances other forces.

What is to be done about these forces, these possibilities, these dangers? Our methods of approaching such problems must be different, more expansive. Albert Einstein may have said it best: "No problem can be solved from the same consciousness that created it. We must learn to see the world anew."[5]

Learning from People with Totally Different Experiences

How do we see the world anew? Of course we need new ideas, and without question we need fundamental change in the ways we have been thinking about and addressing problems. But where do we look for new ideas, and how do we cultivate new ways of thinking? I believe we need to learn in ways that may at first seem unlikely — from those people who are most affected by the ills we have acknowledged: poor, marginalized people, who reside at the bottom of the hierarchies. Their experiences and consciousness are different from those of the people who most often find themselves in positions of leadership.

We all need to learn from the perspectives and ideas of people totally different from ourselves. We need to learn from the "other." Men need to learn from women, whites from blacks, old from young, young from old, rich from poor, educated from illiterate, and so on. If we truly could learn from one another, we might see the world anew. For this reason, I believe that diversity in all aspects of an organization is a key principle for effecting change.

As all of us learn from each other, we will grow to realize that we *are* each other. We are one. Even if we are lucky and never experience oppression, poverty, or violence, some of those around us will not be so lucky: sisters, brothers, daughters, sons, colleagues, and friends who are of color, gay, disabled, non-English speaking, et cetera. I am reminded of this "confession" by a World War II pastor: "First they came for the communists, and I did not speak out because I was not a communist; then they came for the socialists, and I did not speak out because I was not a socialist; then they came for the trade unionists, and I did not speak out because I was not a trade unionist; then they came for the Jews, and I did not speak out because I was not a Jew. Then they came for me, and there was no one left to speak out for me."[6]

What has become abundantly clear with globalization and the internationalization of our everyday lives is that we are no longer separate persons or countries. We are affected by others and are interconnected members of a global community. What happens to and affects one of us affects us all. We need to figure out how to relate to each other in mutually supportive and respectful ways.

I believe that the situation of women worldwide serves as a critical paradigm for creating essential and lasting change in the nature of relationships between and among other groups. Women currently comprise more than 51 percent of the world's population, and we are a vastly untapped resource for positive global transformation. Women's lives — our roles, aspirations, needs, and goals — are shaped by the state of the world. And conversely, women's lives — our poverty, lack of education, and demeaned status — shape the world. Women's perspectives are basic to our seeing the world anew, not because these perspectives are determined by our biology but because our gendered experiences as women in our societies have not been fully heard or integrated into processes of change.

For the most part, women see the world from the bottom of the hierarchical systems in which we live. Although some progress has been made in the last few decades, the economic, social, and human rights situations of most women in today's world continue to be bleak. At this point in human history, according to United Nations sources, there is no major field of activity, whether it be the economy, education, health, or government, and no country in which women have equality with men.[7]

Women worldwide do almost all the world's domestic work, and yet we seldom receive income for the time and effort this work entails. Women provide more health care than all the organized health services put together, and yet many women lack equal access to health care for themselves. Women grow more than half the world's food, yet we own only 1 percent of the world's land. Women make up one-third of the world's paid labor force, yet we are concentrated in the lowest-paid occupations. Women comprise more than 50 percent of the world's population, and yet we are discriminated against in terms of education; there are eighty million more boys than girls enrolled in primary and secondary schools. Women comprise 50 percent of the world's enfranchised population, and yet we hold no more than 10 percent of the seats in national legislatures.

Although most analysts of international development would now agree that development efforts cannot succeed unless the contributions and needs of women are understood and addressed, research on women's roles and status has been greatly neglected.[8] And women's full participation in all walks of life has simply not happened.

Despite these harsh facts, in country after country, women's groups and individual women not only have survived but have become empowered; they have visions for positive change, they have developed plans to reach toward those visions, and they are taking steps to implement their plans. The greenbelt movement in Kenya, the social credit schemes of India, the Argentine "women in black" protesting human rights violations — these are only three examples of thousands of efforts that began modestly and quietly through the efforts of ordinary women and have had far-reaching effects. These efforts to effect change in current paradigms were begun by women for the benefit of their larger societies. Author and peace activist Elise Boulding has emphasized in her writing that women's efforts are carried out not solely for the sake of women but for the general liberation of the human spirit.[9]

It was against this backdrop and with these problems in mind that we created The Global Fund for Women. We had a vision for a changed paradigm, one that would fit the problems and the times. In the first annual report of The Fund, I wrote,

> Our time has been described by Edward Whitmont in *The Return of the Goddess* as a "low point of cultural development that has led us into the deadlock of scientific materialism, technological destructiveness, religious nihilism, and spiritual impoverishment." In such a time, it is both necessary and inevitable that certain values, commonly perceived as "feminine," receive much greater prominence. Around the world, we see both women and men putting into practice such values as nurturing the earth, respecting the cycles of the earth, and expressing a love and concern for the generations that follow.[10]

Many may wonder whether pervasive discrimination and violence against women are inevitable. Writers hark back to early times and matriarchal societies where women apparently enjoyed equal status. But historians have difficulty proving such theories. For my part, I think we need to create new paradigms of organization, paradigms that draw on values such as those referred to just above, whether or not the world has seen such patterns before. Never mind that societies where women had equality may once have existed. The idea is interesting and attractive, but what is more important now, I believe, is answering in the positive these kinds of questions: Can we imagine a world where all women and all men enjoy equality? Can we believe, as I tried to help the student at the post-9/11 panel believe, that there are things we can do to make positive change? Can innovative and viable plans of action emerge from such dreams and beliefs?

Of course I answer these questions with a resounding "yes!" I am one of the lucky people in this world who saw the seed of an idea grow into a real organization, The Global Fund for Women, which has made a positive difference to thousands of people around the world. In my work, I have drawn strength from such thoughts as this, from the Talmud: "Do not be daunted by the enormity of the world's grief. Do justly, now. Love mercy, now. Walk humbly, now. You are not obligated to complete the work, but neither are you free to abandon it." My beliefs have been strengthened by the words and deeds of numerous people from many walks of life, people who have exemplified justice, mercy, and humility in their work.

My hope is that similar beliefs will grow in you and guide you in your efforts for change. Believing that positive change is possible is the beginning. Realizing that you yourself can effect such change will lead you to clarify your vision and identify the skills you need to prepare the ground and plant the seeds of change.

Things to Remember
as You Cultivate Your Dreams

- Believe that change is possible. (See the barren patch of ground and be aware that a garden can grow there.)

- Be good to yourself; allow yourself to envision change.

- Begin to think about specific goals and a possible plan of action, however modest that may be. (A tiny garden can be beautiful.)

- Consciously act in terms of a paradigm that celebrates diversity without categorizing some people as better than others. See the world in terms of *both/and* and *win/win*.

CHAPTER TWO

Be True to Yourself
and Learn

—— ◁◁◯◁◯◯◁◯▷ ——

There is a vitality, a life force, a quickening
That is translated through you into action,
And because there is only one of you in all time,
This expression is unique.
If you block it,
It will never exist through any other medium
And will be lost.
The world will not have it....

— Martha Graham

Back in the mid-1980s, my life, though full and exciting, was a little bit frustrating. The good parts were that my daughter was in law school and living at home, I had taken up yoga, and I had become very active in international development issues. In my work at the Hewlett Foundation, however, I tried each year during my last four years there (1983 to 1987) to interest the president, and through him the board of directors, in developing a women's program. I was sure that enhancing the status of women — we didn't talk about "empowerment" then — was an essential part of all development efforts, particularly programs

19

having to do with population and family planning. But I could not convince them of the importance — even the urgency — of such a program.

For this reason and others, by early 1987 I had begun to lose heart with my job at Hewlett and planned to leave it at the end of the year. Interesting as it had been, I was tired of doing the same things — writing grant descriptions for the board, trying to convince the president and board to fund women's activities, and fielding the same old questions from potential grantees.

One evening that spring, I was having dinner with two women, talking about our futures and the state of the world. It was a Saturday night, March 28, 1987. Frances Kissling, the president of Catholics for a Free Choice, Laura Lederer, an author who was then a program officer at the Skaggs Foundation, and I were attending the Council on Foundations' annual conference, held that year in Philadelphia. As usual, Frances had found a superb restaurant. Over dinner, we began to talk about what I was going to do after I left the Hewlett Foundation.

I remember saying over a glass of champagne, "There is one thing I wanted to do at the Hewlett Foundation before I left, and I haven't accomplished it. I wanted to begin a program of funding women's groups, and I haven't been able to convince the board that this would be a good thing to do. I've given up, and I feel sorry about it." As I recall, Frances responded by suggesting that I start my own foundation so that I could be president and be free to follow my own agenda. "Well," I said, "that would be great. If I had a million dollars, I'd start a foundation that would give grants to women's groups around the world. Too bad, but I don't have that kind of money." Without hesitation Frances countered, "That's no problem. Raise the money from lots of people — people like you and me. Wouldn't you give some money to a group that supported women around the world? We could be on the board and make some grants." Excited by these ideas, we decided to order another bottle of champagne.

Frances and I had a tradition of meeting for good dinners and great discussions. We would kick ideas back and forth. It was always stimulating and lots of fun. Of the many ideas that had surfaced at such dinners, however, this one really grabbed me. I remember leaning forward and musing about who might be involved in such an organization — an international foundation that would raise money to give to women. I even made some notes at the table. And I quickly became obsessed with the idea — so much so that I couldn't sleep that night.

All sorts of thoughts raced through my head: I would start this organization — this international women's foundation — and it would give away ten million dollars by the year 2000. People would be invited to join us in our vision — to strengthen women around the world, to change the way they were being seen and the way they saw themselves, and to do this by getting money into women's hands so that they could carry out their own programs. This organization wouldn't be bureaucratic. We would listen to the women who were building programs, and we would respond to them rather than set agendas for them to follow. No such organization existed in the world of philanthropy.

The next morning, I had breakfast with Dame Nita Barrow, who had convened the Non-Governmental Organization (NGO) Forum on Women, held in tandem with the United Nations Third World Conference on Women in 1985 in Nairobi, Kenya. Nita was a warm and wonderful Barbadian and a former nurse, with all the wisdom and healing powers that profession promises.

I told her about the idea that we had discussed the night

before and about my excitement. "Let me get this straight, Anne," she said. "You want to create a pool of money to give away to women so that they can do what they want to do and not what the donors want them to do. Is that right?" I said, "Yes, essentially that's the idea." And she said, "If you do this, it will be important. It will make a difference to women. And I will support you in this work." "Don't speak too rashly," I countered. "Will you become a board member?" Nita immediately said, "Yes, and not in name only." This is how Dame Nita Barrow became The Global Fund's fourth founding board member.

Later that morning, after speaking with Nita, I found myself saying to friends and colleagues at the conference, "Some of us are thinking of creating an international foundation that would benefit women." By the afternoon, I was saying, "We're planning to create an international foundation that will benefit women." And by the evening, the words became, "We have created an international foundation that will benefit women." It was just that simple and playful. I was making it up as I went along.

So it was that The Global Fund for Women began. Nita's words had helped to empower me: I felt driven, filled with conviction, and alive. I talked up my dreams at that Council on Foundations meeting, and with enthusiastic feedback from almost everyone I spoke with, I began to feel that something real might come of these ideas.

Recognizing That the Readiness Is All

Many books on starting businesses emphasize that a successful new enterprise almost always necessitates having at least one person involved who is driven, who will do anything to make the organization happen, no matter what. Others might say that things happen to people at just the right times in their lives if they are open to possibilities. I definitely was open to new ideas and opportunities at the time; I was about to go through a transition in my own working life. Also, I was feeling free of the direct responsibilities of a family; I was a single mother, but my daughter, Gwyn, was just finishing law school and she already had a job lined up. In retrospect, I can now see how my experiences before creating The Global Fund for Women prepared me for the work.

I came to understand that some of the impetus to create an organization that would benefit women was very personal. I realized that I was quietly angry, not only because of my growing feeling that many international policy and development programs were screwed up and ineffective — being carried out in ways that wasted money and made no sense, ways that expressed the donors' notions of what was needed as opposed to the ideas of people at the grass roots or directly affected by the programs — but also because of my own personal experiences as a woman.

I had spent years apologizing for and making allowances for various men in my life. I had fought a losing battle with at least one supervisor over a salary that had been described as "a good salary for a woman" but that was not equal to the salaries of the men on the staff who were doing exactly the same work as I was. (Suing for equal pay was an absurd notion that long ago.) I had piled up numerous other experiences of disempowerment and discrimination, some as simple as not being able to get a credit card in my own name after my divorce, some as complicated as having sex with a man because he assumed it rather than because I truly wanted it. My upbringing didn't allow me to express anger directly. It wasn't ladylike; it did not befit a "nice" girl. As it turned out, the creation of an organization that focused on women's issues and women's equality became both a very personal expression of and a great outlet for my feelings.

Sometimes hindsight provides clarity that we don't have in real time. I can now trace a trajectory in my life that makes starting The Global Fund seem almost inevitable. But, of course, it was not inevitable. After the dinner with Frances and Laura, I could have chalked up my enthusiasm to the champagne. I could have said that the idea was a good one but just too daunting. I could have been discouraged by all the things I did not know how to do.

You may doubt yourself when the contours of an innovative action plan begin to form in your mind. You may put the idea aside thinking that your dream is too big. You may ask, "Why me?" I share the following biographical information to answer these questions for myself — and to encourage you to understand not only your motivations but also your credentials. You may have much to learn, as I did, but your vision is likely to be the result of the timeliness and rightness of your inspiration.

One of the many moments that I now believe led to my later actions on behalf of women was an interchange with my mother that took place back in 1955, during my last year at University of California, Berkeley. A researcher who had studied the aspirations and qualifications of undergraduate students, one of whom was me, had suggested that I consider getting a graduate degree. I told my mother about this over a cup of tea in the kitchen one afternoon. Mum counseled me to not "get too educated"; she thought that doing so would work against my marrying, something that had worked out happily for her and had served as a successful route out of a difficult childhood situation. She believed that I, too, should link up with a man who would look after me and care for me all of my life. Her advice was offered with love, keeping what she sincerely felt were my best interests in mind; she was trying to help me navigate the world in the way she knew best. Years later, when I traveled internationally and learned about bound feet, genital mutilation, and other limitations imposed upon girls for the most part by women, I understood that mothers participate in such things with loving intent, hoping to give their daughters a better chance in the world as they see it. I listened to my mother and agreed — and did not pursue a graduate degree until I was in my late thirties.

My upbringing and early life also contributed to my sense of injustice, particularly in the different ways the sexes are treated. Tagging along behind my brother and his friends, I was always conscious of the fact that Bob was going to be able to do certain adventurous things and I was not. Later, when the family moved to New Zealand and I was in my early teens, I entered an all-girl public school, and I no longer had to cope with the boys' teasing. In this single-sex school, I had wonderful female role models in the teachers, the administrators, and the students who served in class government. I experienced, in fact, a small world where everyone in charge was female. After moving to California, I spent the last two years of high school back in a coed school where girls competed for boys' attention. But I was very active and very empowered; I ran for treasurer of my new school with the campaign slogan, "Do you want your money manhandled or woman-handled?" (Because of or in spite of this slogan, I was elected.)

I graduated from high school with an eye toward traveling and eventually working at the United Nations. Given the dominant influence of the Second World War in my childhood and family, I believed that the United Nations was the hope for the world. I applied and was accepted to the University of California, Berkeley, where I majored in political science and economics. I graduated three years later — I was in a hurry to get out, work, and see the world — and I applied and was accepted for a two-month UN internship.

When I went to New York for the summer of 1955, as the youngest UN intern in a group of about thirty people from as many countries, a good number of us applied for jobs in the 1955 General Assembly. I was hired as a documents clerk. Unlike the male interns, we girls were not considered for professional jobs. We were equally qualified but were told to apply only for positions as clerks, secretaries, or guides. Virtually no women worked as professionals at the United Nations at that time, and such discrimination continued for decades. All of this seemed unfair to me, but it was just "the way it was."

What's more, although there was no word for it in my early twenties, virtually every young woman I knew suffered sexual harassment or abuse. I worked in the basement in the documents section of the United Nations, and the delegates and their minions would come down to pick up documents — and flirt. Their comments and conversational gambits were inappropriate, demeaning, and confusing. (Were we girls somehow asking for it, we wondered?) During the following General Assembly, in 1956, when I was working for the delegation from Ceylon (now Sri Lanka) and was frequently upstairs in the delegate's lounge at the United Nations, the level of harassment was even more pronounced. Sometimes my roommates and I would talk about these incidents, but we couldn't call it what it was — sexual harassment — and in our ignorance and innocence we thought that such disturbing treatment was normal between older men and younger women.

My life as a young married woman was also filled with many confusions and disappointments that lacked names and were only beginning to be understood in a framework of sexual inequality. I felt I couldn't choose to retain my maiden name when I married, and so "Anne Firth" suddenly seemed no longer to exist. And when the unsatisfactory contraceptive technology of the time failed, I became pregnant before I and my husband were ready to have a child.

As a young mother, I came across *The Feminine Mystique* by Betty Friedan.[1] Although it didn't describe my situation exactly, it was close enough for discomfort. I bought several copies and sent them to my friends, many of whom were at home looking after toddlers. How the book resonated with us! This was in the early 1960s, but we were living with the legacy of the 1950s, when media messages were telling us to be perfect Betty Crocker cooks, happy homemakers, and cheerful helpmates — while the greater world assigned little value to these roles.

Ultimately, my own personal experiences as a woman sharpened and deepened my understanding of the central importance of the roles of women in the issues I was working on professionally in the 1980s at the Hewlett Foundation — international development, population and family planning, and environmental and conservation issues. My interest in doing something about the state of the world and the problems that pestered me as I read the daily newspaper became very personal. I wanted to change the world for people less fortunate than I, and I wanted to change it for women like me too.

I think of my high school and college times and especially my UN internship experience when I speak to the students in my classes at Stanford. They are idealistic and eager to change the world, as I was. They want to contribute. There is such intensity and longing to be relevant, to be of use. Such enthusiasm can be dampened by experience, responsibility, disappointments, and the realities of our world. But we can revive it when we remind ourselves that change is possible and that we ourselves can take action.

Learning All the Time

When The Global Fund for Women began in 1987, although I was more than fifty years old, I felt very much like a person in the first phase of life. It was a time of learning, a time of acquiring skills, a time of clarifying beliefs, a time of being a student again. These activities, so appropriate for young people in the first third of their lives, also became very appropriate for me as I began to put together The Global Fund for Women.

Yes, I had years of experience creating foundation programs, serving on boards, developing successful grant-making programs, convening meetings, writing, and editing. But I knew next to nothing about raising money or creating an organization from scratch. Yes, I had managed staffs in previous jobs, but my hope was to create systems of management that would be different from the predictable structures of other organizations. I knew little of computer technology, but I wanted this women's organization to be at the forefront of that technology. Of course I had developed some deeply held values, but could they be applied to the organization as it grew? As this organization began to sprout from the seed of an idea, a vision, to become a little seedling, I needed help and greater knowledge.

In those early days, my friend Barry Rose and my cofounder, Frances, provided such help. They were available by telephone (email was not common then) to discuss whatever I needed to talk about. Barry was a good sounding board, a wise and interested listening post, as well as a constant supporter. Frances, a fountain of ideas, also located a law firm in Washington DC to create the legal documents for the organization, while I, in California, found office space, a computer, and a printer (all donated), and some base money to get started. During The Global Fund's first eighteen months of life, in 1987 and 1988, I devoted my nights and my weekends to it, while I continued to work full-time for pay at the Hewlett Foundation and later as a regents lecturer at the University of California, San Francisco. Very soon others joined us in our vision, and I was challenged to find ways to make wise use of the many people who asked, "What can I do to help?"

As the idea and the organization grew, there was still much to be learned. Past experience had given me background in organizational development, and to gain knowledge about how to raise money to sustain an organization, I read books, I signed up for a course or two, and I found some excellent mentors.

I knew that creating a new organization would require me to speak often in public; I had to learn how to do that well too. My early terror of public speaking was such that I once became sick and had to be taken home before I was due to make a speech at a high school assembly in New Zealand! But at my California high school, I decided to join the speech club. As an assignment, I wrote a speech, straight from my heart, about why I supported the United Nations. I believed in what I wrote, memorized my words, delivered them — and won my school's speech award that year. That experience allayed my paralyzing fear of public speaking, but I still approached microphones and audiences with sweaty palms and a lump in my throat. I needed to gain confidence in speaking often and with ease.

Those of us hoping to bring about change needn't become fearless speakers, and we don't have to memorize our speeches.

But we do need to articulate our visions and plans in order to involve and inspire others. I soon learned that if I knew clearly what I was trying to do and why — if I could speak from the heart and view public speech as communication rather than performance — this would go a long way toward ensuring success. I also picked up other tips along the way: start small, by speaking up in small groups; give some thought to how you organize your words and to whom you are speaking; identify the common ground you know you have with your listeners, ask questions, involve others; and tell personal stories. Because I observed that women often held back in public meetings, I vowed that I would speak out more often at such gatherings, first figuring out something useful to say and then having the courage to raise my hand and make my point.

I also took a one-day class in public speaking, and it vastly improved my ability to stand in front of an audience and speak honestly and clearly. In the class, I learned some quite simple lessons: wear comfortable shoes and a familiar outfit rather than something new that you have just acquired; stand evenly on both feet; hold your arms open rather than closed across your chest (open arms express more open communication); slow down; tell a little story at the beginning of your talk — something that connects you to your audience, not necessarily a joke — and make eye contact with people in the audience. With regard to the talk itself: know clearly what three or four main points you want to communicate to your audience; tell your listeners at the beginning what those points are; in the main part of your talk, describe these points in more detail; and at the end, very briefly summarize these points again. Finish your talk with a suggestion of something that people in the audience can do, something that may spur them to action.

Communication skills are important — in fact, key — if one is planning to create a healthy organization. At least I had expertise in the written word, a skill that I honed as an editor at Oxford, Yale, and Stanford University Presses, at the Institute of International Studies in Berkeley, and at the United Nations, where, in the 1970s, I finally attained a position as a writer and editor.

However, I was bothered by my lack of foreign language skills. In creating The Global Fund, I was presuming to create an international organization, one that I hoped would span the globe and reach women in every country (as, indeed, The Global Fund for Women has done). How could I, a person fluent only in my own language, presume to lead such an organization? I wondered and sometimes felt inadequate, but I was driven and I moved forward, albeit monolingually. Nevertheless, my first suggestion to students and others who wish to change the world these days is to become fluent in at least one and preferably more than one other language. I can get by in quite a few languages — if I am lost, I can find my way back to the hotel — but I feel that I have missed a major experience in life by not being truly fluent in a language other than English. Perhaps it is not too late.

Despite the limitations on my language ability, travel in various parts of the world has always been part of my life. When I reached age twenty-one, the year my parents deemed it acceptable for me to travel alone, I went to Europe for ten months, determined to survive on my own meager funds, taking jobs as needed. I decided to begin in England, where I could speak the language. Later I ventured to France and other parts of Europe and learned that I was pretty good at communicating with people using my college French and lots of gestures.

It was unusual at that time for a girl my age to be traveling alone. There were no credit cards, no cell phones, no palm pilots, no Internet cafés, and my parents must have worried terribly. (I still recall their advice to me on the day before I was to set sail from New York: "Eat well and stay healthy; don't scrimp on this. If you ever feel frightened or in trouble, go to the best hotel in town and wire us collect.") I felt like a golden girl with the world at my feet on the ship en route to Europe. Shipboard students invited me to their countries and homes. I saw most of Western Europe, staying with friends and their families, traveling by train and bus, and hitchhiking occasionally. It was a freeing, empowering adventure; I began to see the world in new ways. I think now of André Gide's belief that "One does not discover new lands without consenting to lose sight of the shore for a very long time."[2] The freedom that I experienced in Europe and the welcoming families I met confirmed my positive view of the world and of people. I was a trusting soul, and my trust was not betrayed. I came away confirmed in my belief that people are basically good and generous. (I was also happy to learn that in different parts of the world, different standards of female beauty prevail. On my trip, I learned to appreciate my Rubenesque body type, an important thing for a young woman then and now.)

Work and travel led me to Hong Kong in 1958, where I took a job teaching English at Chung Chi College, so my limited language abilities did not hamper me too much there either. Still, I consider my lack of verbal language skill not just a liability in our global world today but a missed opportunity to see the world through the eyes of others. My daughter, who speaks three languages fluently, says that different languages enable her to see not only the world but herself in different ways.

In order to give reality to our dreams of social justice, we need to be able to clearly articulate our vision, goals, and plans as we write proposals and fund-raising letters and communicate by email and other new mediums. We need to learn to write well, to communicate in many languages, and to speak in public with ease.

What about formal learning, going to university, doing graduate work? When my mother told me not to get too educated for fear that I might not catch a husband, I took her seriously and didn't return to university until the mid-1970s, when I was in my late thirties. It was hard to go back to school at that age, as a single mother with a young daughter living in New York. I wish that I had been able to do graduate study earlier, perhaps a year or two after completing my undergraduate work in the mid-1950s. If you are casting about for what to do, formal learning — honing skills, learning languages, gaining new perspectives, going to college or university — is a great thing to do while you are looking for your passion. If in doubt or despair, learn something!

Moving Quickly from Dreams to Reality

When a vision forms, take action soon to make your dreams real. Early on at The Global Fund for Women, we began to clarify the values of the organization, believing that our guiding principles should be understandable and publishable. We also began to build the board of directors and staff; by the spring of 1988, just a year after the inspirational dinner with Frances and Laura, The Global Fund had added two more board members, two staff members (I had hired a part-time administrator and a part-time grants manager), and a couple of interns. And to demonstrate what we wanted to do, in June of 1988 we made seven small grants that could serve as examples of our vision and goals.

It may seem that we moved very quickly to make our vision real. But there was method to our madness. At the conference in

Philadelphia, where we had first talked about creating a new organization, I quickly began to speak of our creation as if it were real, as if it already existed. I find this to be a useful strategy. It is strengthening to give reality to your dreams as soon as possible. The statement "We have created an organization that will benefit women" is much stronger than "We hope to create such an organization."

Many people have asked me: "How did you actually start a new organization? How did you start The Global Fund for Women?" My answer is usually something like this: "I just began. We just did what needed to be done." In moving forward to actually create a program, even though your actions may be modest, keep in mind Henry David Thoreau's dictum: "For it matters not how small the beginning may seem to be; what is once well done is done forever."[3] In short, *there is no beginning too small!* Perhaps your first steps will be small, but at least you begin, you do something. You begin drawing upon your own experience, and you quickly find out what you need to learn. The key for us was that we needed to implement our program (making grants) very soon, in order to demonstrate clearly to potential donors what we were all about and how we planned to do our work, as well as to energize ourselves by the very reality of the actions.

The style of The Global Fund, which ultimately distinguished it from other organizations, was very personal. I wanted to look forward to going to work each day. I wanted the organization to be the way I wanted the world to be: friendly, modest, diverse, honest, generous, respectful, loving, fair, efficient, and effective. I feel the same way about my classes at Stanford.

This drive to characterize the organization — and, indeed, other environments in which I live and work — in terms of a set of values or principles that always include respect, equality, diversity, and fairness can be partly explained, I think, by my heritage as a New Zealander. The New Zealand into which I was born was proudly described as a welfare state; it was a system, as my father used to explain, based on the "right of all people" to education and health care from "the womb to the tomb." The Maori people, who sailed to New Zealand from the Pacific Islands long before the English settlers arrived, were not conquered when the English colonized New Zealand. They fought and they were not defeated, and they signed the Treaty of Waitangi to become British subjects under Queen Victoria as equals under the law. The way this history was presented to me by my family and in school in New Zealand caused me to believe that New Zealand was a land of full equality. Certainly that was the ideal and still is. But now, decades later, individual rights have come to the fore and we see major changes, pain, and some advancements, as decisions made in colonial times have been challenged in fundamental ways. New Zealand, like many other countries, suffered because of a hierarchical and racist colonial mindset.

Nevertheless, I was greatly influenced by the ideal that was presented in my family by my parents. My mother had grown up living among Maori families in what turned out to be my birthplace, Wanganui, and her mother spoke fluent Maori. My father was from a working class family; his father was a railway worker. I believe that my fascination with the experiences of others — people different from myself — began in my childhood, in a family where at parties the local grocer, a visiting student, and a university professor could be equally comfortable in my parents' home. All were treated with respect and in an evenhanded way. And, who knows? Perhaps the fact that New Zealand was the first country in which women had the right to vote (a right granted in 1893) had an influence on my later interests.

By the time I was born in June 1935, my father was rising

through the government service ranks and was posted to Los Angeles as the Trade and Tourist Commissioner for New Zealand. The first three years of my life were spent in Los Angeles, leaving me with a clear California accent! From there we moved to Canada where, with the exception of a year or so in Washington DC, we stayed for eight years. My father was then Acting High Commissioner for New Zealand in Canada, and we led a somewhat privileged life. But the Second World War dominated our lives; my mother worked with the Red Cross and my father coordinated training programs for New Zealand airmen in transit through Canada on their way to Europe. Throughout those war years, at school in Canada, we children were taught to be useful, to knit woolen squares to sew together into blankets for "the boys" overseas, to save every scrap of metal, even silver paper, to contribute to the war effort, and to respect food rationing. Some of my favorite New Zealand airmen, who had spent holidays with our family when they came for training in Canada, died in Europe. Our parents did not talk openly about the deaths in Europe, but somehow my brother and I knew what had happened from their silence and sadness.

At each stage in our family life, my parents instilled in me the idea that we were lucky. We were reminded of our good fortune when Dad and Mum would make the point that, unlike others, my father had a job during the Depression. And during the war, we were lucky to be in Canada and not in England, where our cousins were being bombed. My parents implied and sometimes said aloud that we therefore were more responsible for the needs of others. Being lucky brought with it an obligation to become involved, to give. The strong sense that I am a lucky person and therefore responsible to those less fortunate is at the base of my commitment to bettering the world.

Since you are reading this book, I suspect you share my commitment to positive social change. Not everyone is lucky enough to feel empowered to serve others and the world community. But I believe that most people do find meaning through such service. The mantras on true love from Thich Nhat Hanh — "Dear One: I am here for you" and "Dear One: I know that you are suffering; that is why I am here for you"[4] — express this. Of course there are times in our lives when it is impossible for us to reach out and be there for others; we may need others to be there for us. At such times we need to be strong enough to say, as Thich Nhat Hanh counsels, "Dear one. I am suffering so much. Help me please." Can we get to a point, I wonder, where we all can be as open with each other as this?

When the student challenged the panel of faculty members after September 11, 2001, this is what I was trying to say to her: Reach out to others, and be there for them. Be there for people you know and for others whom you do not know or who may be very different from yourself. And ask for help if you need it. To do this is empowering.

Dear reader — whether you are someone who wants to make the world a better place and are looking for ways to focus this desire, or you are a person with a specific dream for positive change and want help to organize such an effort — others are there for you. By sharing my experience of bringing to reality a dream for a better world, I hope to provide some help to you, perhaps some inspiration. Know that you can bring about change and know that you can learn.

There are many ways to be there for others; all are important. There is no hierarchy for effecting positive change. Knowing that change is possible is the beginning. Feeling your own power to make change is next. Look to your own experience and background to find the heartfelt context for your work. Creating an effective organization, program, or campaign requires connecting the head and the heart, the intellectual rationale for the work and the heartfelt passion to make change happen.

Looking back, I see that the years and many of the personal experiences that had preceded my time at the Hewlett Foundation combined to give me the experience, knowledge, and passion that resulted in my feeling driven and empowered to create The Global Fund for Women.

Things to Remember
as You Cultivate Your Dreams

- Assess and value your own principles and skills.

- Always learn. "The best thing for being sad ... is to learn something. That is the only thing that never fails. You may grow old and trembling in your anatomies; you may see the world around you devastated by evil lunatics, or know your honor trampled in the sewers of baser minds. There is only one thing for it then — to learn." — T. H. White, *The Once and Future King*[5]

- Do not be afraid to ask for help.

- Listen to your heart and your head. Recall, with James Stephens, the Irish poet, that "the head does not hear anything until the heart has listened, and what the heart knows today the head will understand tomorrow.... If you listen to your heart, you will learn every good thing, for the heart is the fountain of wisdom."[6]

CHAPTER THREE

Connect to Build Trust and Freedom

Never doubt that a small group of thoughtful, committed citizens can change the world. Indeed, it is the only thing that ever has.

— Margaret Mead

My time at the Hewlett Foundation, from 1978 through 1987, provided me with experience to move forward, but the work also highlighted some of the disconnects that I found myself wanting to address as I contemplated leaving and creating a new organization. As we will explore in this chapter, I became increasingly sure that effecting positive change requires making connections of all kinds. I saw that the seemingly simple act of people connecting, coming together, and sharing their experience is a powerful force. I also understood that issues are inextricably linked to an underlying web of contexts and causes.

In 1987, before leaving the foundation, I took part in an evaluation of a clinic in a rural village outside of Ife, Nigeria. My visit coincided with the day that the women from smaller villages were gathering to have their monthly meeting. Some forty women arrived on foot, on bicycles, and on mopeds — all carrying black bags, filled with the supplies and medications they needed on their village rounds delivering primary health care and information on family planning. As I watched them arrive and greet one another, I felt their energy and goodwill toward one another.

They were coming together to share all that they had seen and learned. With tremendous empathy, they discussed the stories of the many women in the small villages where they lived and worked. In one case, they talked about a woman who had not used contraception and therefore had had another baby, her eighth. They spoke about how it was too much for her — she had had a miscarriage and was bleeding — and how they did their best to help her. They spoke of young girls who had become pregnant and had tried to abort their fetuses in an unsafe manner, causing the girls to bleed and sometimes die. They spoke of the times that they were able to help and the times that their help was not enough. Every day these women dealt with the basics of life and death. They were there for the village women. Their commitment was clear. They were being paid almost nothing to do this, yet they remained on the front line, striving to do something.

As I quietly listened to the translator and observed the women, I felt and saw how important these monthly meetings were for the women; they were strengthened and renewed by coming together, by knowing and trusting each other, by connecting. Although I was an outsider, I was immediately welcomed, introduced, and brought into the dancing, the singing, and the role playing that the women used as they shared their work and their learning.

Meeting and Introducing

As I began to work more and more with women's groups around the world, I was struck by how different their meetings were from those that I was accustomed to. On a trip through Southeast Asia in 1992, I met with grantees and then attended a regional meeting in Singapore, which included about twenty people, to discuss possible bases for collaboration. At the very beginning of the meeting, plenty of time, perhaps two hours, was spent allowing each person to introduce herself and to speak about her dreams for the outcome of the meeting. In this way, a trusting atmosphere was created, each person was carefully included, and our mutual vision for change could begin to emerge. Often at such meetings we sat on the floor, in a circle, so we could all see and hear each other.

Meeting, connecting, and hearing each other is important in order to create an atmosphere of trust in which diverse people can feel comfortable sharing their varied perspectives. Because it is essential that we begin to learn from others very different from ourselves in order to appropriately address the major issues of our time and see the world anew, we must feel safe in our surroundings so that we can express our true thoughts and beliefs.

What a contrast such women's meetings were to those at which I represented the Hewlett Foundation! I recall one meeting in particular — a donors' meeting, held at the International Planned Parenthood Federation in London sometime in the late 1970s. About twenty-five people were in attendance, all seated around a huge long table. Each participant identified herself or himself very briefly by name and organization, with the exception of six or seven people — all women — seated near the very end of the table. These were the secretaries, the administrative staff, who had typed and compiled the documents, who were there to get us refreshments, who were there to handle a multitude of details. I was very new to the international donor world at that time, but I was embarrassed by this lapse, and I remember screwing up my courage, raising my hand, and saying that we had neglected to introduce everyone in the room. With surprise and a little chagrin, the chairperson turned to the women who shyly but happily introduced themselves.

The practice of including only the seemingly important people in a meeting is not a thing of the past. Think of recent meetings that you have attended. Was everyone included or at least introduced? Have you ever been at a meeting where you did not feel free to express your opinion, especially if it differed from the views that dominated the discussion? I recently went to a small meeting, with only about a dozen participants, where initial introductions were simply forgotten. I felt hesitant to suggest that we all introduce ourselves — although I did — because I was not the convener of the meeting. But I am now so used to this feminist tradition of including and connecting that I find it awkward to be in a meeting where we all haven't at least voiced our names and said something about ourselves at the very beginning.

At The Global Fund for Women, we sought to start each meeting by having everyone speak, however briefly. I remember a meeting in Beijing with at least sixty representatives from grantee groups, yet we asked everyone to introduce herself and say a few words. It took some time, but the sheer diversity of the group was inspiring and moving. *Dalit* (untouchable) women from south Asia stood next to women from higher castes; poor women stood beside richer ones, all proudly saying their names and something about the work that their groups were doing. The sense of unity in diversity was palpable. The sense of something greater than each individual set the tone for the meeting and excited us all.

What if we are convening a meeting where there are just too many people to introduce? It is always possible to take a minute or two at the beginning of any meeting, even if there are a hundred people in attendance, to ask everyone to turn to the people on either side of them, briefly exchange introductions, and perhaps ask a probing question of each other. Making efforts to include everyone in an evenhanded way results in a sense of cohesion and connection, rather than fragmentation, and it can build trust and lead to the freedom and openness so basic to innovation.

Working Together and Building Trust

E. M. Forster was referring to the dual natures of human beings when he wrote in *Howard's End*, "Only connect the prose and the passion, and both will be exalted.... Live in fragments no longer."[1] But these words express what became a constant theme as The Global Fund developed. One of our earliest beliefs, which was quickly transformed into a guiding principle, was that people meeting and working together, rather than alone, are a powerful force for change. Whenever I was in doubt about an action, I would opt for the path that would bring people together rather than separate them. I came to believe that the act of coming together rather than separating ourselves is basic to positive social change. This principle was demonstrated often by the women who sought support from The Global Fund for Women.

A typical letter from a women's group to The Fund would begin something like this: "We are three women in a village in Nigeria. We are concerned that women who are street vendors do not have any way to get health or medical care. Their children need care, and so do the women. They have asked us to help them create a health clinic near where they work. Will you help us?" We would write back seeking to learn more about what the women planned to do, how they planned to do it, and why they thought their group was particularly qualified to carry out the plan. By the time the women had come to the point of writing to The Fund, they had created a small community and begun to develop a plan. Now they needed to expand their group by writing to us, reaching out to other women, contacting medical people, and so on.

I remember a request from some university researchers in Korea who had been studying social behavior and had been stunned by what they were learning about levels of domestic violence in their city. They wrote something like this: "We are five women sociologists who have been doing research on family relations. We have learned that the problem of domestic abuse is widespread in Korea. We have met with some social workers and some women who have experienced abuse, and we have heard of 'hotlines' that women in other countries have started where women who need advice and help can get it. Can you help us?" We wrote back encouraging them and asking them to tell us more about their plans; from that early inquiry and a small grant came the first domestic abuse center in Korea.

Was there some special magic about a few women coming together to discuss a problem and then finding the strength to do something about it? We marveled at how many requests came from just three women or five women. No matter what the number, it was almost invariably a small group of women who had been worried about a problem and then, through conversation and sharing ideas, they would find the strength — the empowerment — to begin to do something about that problem. (As you will recall, The Global Fund for Women had its beginnings during a dinner discussion of three women too.) Connecting with others is energizing and empowering.

This practice of connection and inclusion works very well in my classes at Stanford too, where, on the first day of class, each student introduces herself or himself and repeats the name of every other student. During the early weeks in class, students meet in smaller groups to learn more about each other, and they visit me at my home for tea. As I explain at the beginning of each class, I want to try to create a community in the class, even if we are together for only ten weeks. In these classes, we are talking about serious international issues related to women's health and human rights — issues such as unwanted pregnancy, HIV/AIDS, and intimate-partner abuse — that often affect students very personally. It is important to be able to discuss the topics openly, in a trusting manner, with the thought that individually and collectively we can make a difference.

Some may ask, "Why should students get to know each other to the point where we may care about each other, about women in Nigeria, about poor people in Los Angeles, or about human rights in Korea?" What is the point? One answer that may seem cryptic is "because those people are us." We are one. We are intricately connected. The global epidemic of HIV/AIDS and the potential plague of avian flu are good examples of our connections and interdependence, but there are many other examples, as communications and transport networks crisscross the globe and every country becomes multicultural and internationalized. As this happens, we are faced with the possibility of feeling separated from each other at the very same time as we have the means to come closer and create community. We need to consciously find ways to interact with each other in order to include, connect, and create community.

Connecting Ideas

It is clear to me now how my early experiences in life paved the way for my building The Global Fund for Women. I also see how the insights and experience gained at the Hewlett Foundation added to that path. At the time that I took the Hewlett Foundation job, in 1978, I was in need of connection and stability, having just been divorced and living as a single mother in New York. The job suited me perfectly, bringing me back to the San Francisco Bay Area, where I had family and friends, and providing me with what turned out to be an interesting training ground for developing the vision and systems of The Global Fund.

At the Hewlett Foundation, I ran the population and environment programs. From the beginning, the population program was to be international in its scope; in contrast, the environment program focused on issues in the United States. This disconnect struck me as odd, and I spent quite a lot of time trying to define the connections between the population and environment programs and bring them together. This was to no avail. The programs remained separate, and ultimately the responsibility of the environment program was passed on to a new colleague.

Concentrating on the population and reproductive health program, I traveled widely and learned constantly about other kinds of connections, particularly from women at village and grassroots levels. I found, for example, that among many of the groups that the foundation had supported through U.S.-based intermediaries were family planning centers that had gone well beyond their narrow focus on contraception and family planning to include the creation of groups where women would meet to talk and learn new skills or begin some sort of income-producing activity. Again and again, I saw women participating in these activities first and then becoming interested in the family planning activities afterward. To the extent that they were allowed to do so under the terms of the various grants, I saw that women were defining their own needs and responding to them, despite the grant rather than directly because of it. Their needs often involved chances to come together, to meet and share their lives, to determine what activities would be most useful to them and to their communities.

For example, I remember traveling in Nepal on one occasion in 1996 and visiting a rural village where the United Nations was implementing a relatively new program to promote income generation. When I asked the women of the village about the income-generating program and its perceived value, they responded by saying that it was interesting and possibly useful, but far more important was to increase understanding between men and women and increase people's sense of the value of each other. As it turned out, that income-generating program was discontinued after two years, when the donor concluded that no significant measurable results relating to the terms of the grant had been observed. But the program had resulted in the women getting together to talk and share their concerns, and they had created a local community center with a health clinic and a program of regular women's meetings.

In another case, while visiting a program in Mombasa, Kenya, which the Hewlett Foundation had funded through an intermediate organization, I came upon a group of very strong women who had an interesting approach to using grant money. In the course of conversation, they explained that they had done what the intermediate donor had told them to do with the money but that they had also begun something that they considered far more important — programs to convene women to discuss their problems and their perceptions of appropriate solutions. At the time, representatives of donor agencies were pushing the expansion of family planning clinics because it fitted their larger agenda of population control. Meanwhile, women on the ground argued that primary health care, domestic abuse programs, and access to paid employment were their greatest priorities. Finding out about such differences in priority involved one-on-one conversations with women at the village level, women who had nothing to lose by expressing their opinions. Unlike the village women, the more educated and more economically secure women and men who held positions either in donor agencies or in agencies that were dependent on foreign donors more often expressed views that mirrored those of the outside donors. It was during that visit to Mombasa in particular that I began to dream of a way to connect with and get money directly into the hands of women at the grass roots so that they could do what they wanted to do rather than what the donors — through their project- and program-specific grants — wanted them to do. More and more I saw that women at the village or community level had clear and workable ideas very appropriate to their needs.

Yet, even up to 1987, when my time with the Hewlett Foundation was drawing to an end, and when I was working ever more closely with the international donors in the population field, there was almost no recognition of what had become so evident to me and a few others: that working in the population and family planning field necessitated supporting programs run by women and devised by women. (A notable exception to this generalization was the Ford Foundation, which was working with women at university and policy levels on related issues.) This meant somehow connecting with such women and their local groups, learning from them, and respecting their ideas about effecting real change.

Connecting, in other words, also meant "connecting the dots," figuring out what made sense and learning how to proceed with the people closest to the problems. In order to do that, we needed to create structures that allowed for trusting interchange; we needed to provide much more flexible funding. During an evaluation trip to Nigeria for a major government donor, I asked one of the most impressive program leaders in that country whether he could use extra money in the next grant from the agency. He replied, "I suppose I could think up ways to use more money, but more money is not what we need. We need flexibility. We need the donor's trust in our judgment to take advantage of unusual opportunities and to use the money in possibly unexpected ways for the best outcome. Rather than more money, I ask for greater flexibility and trust."

Again and again, women that I met around the world argued that, although they admired the intentions of most donors, what they wanted was a trusting relationship that would allow them to use grant money more efficiently in terms of their own agendas and not in terms of agendas that were set by agencies far away. Family planning programs were all very well and sometimes useful, but without transportation or child care, women could not get to the clinics; without a source of income, women were marginalized; without education, women were unable to provide effective care. Project-specific funding, often focusing narrowly on family planning only, allowed for no such flexibility. People administering these programs gradually realized that they had to learn from the women if they wanted their programs to be effective.

By 2002, this kind of bottom-up empowerment had become a hot development topic, mostly because of the efforts that had been made by women's groups at the UN International Conference on Population and Development, held in Cairo in 1994. Back in the early 1980s, however, agencies were still setting agendas from the top down, with very few, if any, opportunities to create connection, openness, and real trust between givers and receivers.

In the meantime, the Hewlett Foundation was a model of some good grant-making, despite its lack of interest in supporting women's programs. The fact is that the Hewlett Foundation was one of the very few U.S.-based foundations that consistently offered grantees "flexible general support," meaning money that supported the organization and its programs generally rather than specifying narrow programs or projects. This was one of the greatest lessons that I learned at the Hewlett Foundation — the importance of general support money. Such funds provide freedom and flexibility, which grantees need. And to provide such support effectively, you must connect with grantees, bridge the gap between giver and receiver, and develop trusting relationships.

At The Global Fund for Women, we instituted this general support approach in all of the grants we gave. As I wrote in the report on the fifth year of the life of The Global Fund (1991–92),

[T]he process of empowerment is delicate and creative; it needs space and freedom to succeed. One of the ways in which we promote empowerment of individual women and women's groups...therefore, is by providing flexible general support funds with as little bureaucratic interference as possible, given the need for accountability. For new groups and groups in chaotic and changing societies, this approach is especially important. The less direction a funder imposes, the more free and empowered the grantee is, and the more effective she can be.

I went on to write,

We at The Global Fund need strength and empowerment too, and we receive much from the grantees and volunteers, who remind us that we are not isolated as we work to better society. We also receive strength from our donors — especially those who trusted us at the very beginning with flexible funds for the first steps toward our plans and vision.

The effort was consistent: Always connect. Avoid fragmentation. Create community and trust.

In time, I became particularly interested in the integrative approach that the General Service Foundation was taking, and in 1987 I joined that organization as an outside board member. The interests of the General Service Foundation were peace, environmental concerns, and population matters. In a very modest attempt to recognize the relationships among these issues, the foundation began to fund programs through organizations that worked directly with grassroots communities to address problems at local levels through integrated programs of education, primary health activities, family planning, and agricultural development. People were being trained in leadership skills and community development; family planning, for example, was being taught in the context of reforestation, in the context of alternatives for women, in the context of preservation of the environment and good water use, and so on.

These were the kinds of programs that I hoped that the Hewlett Foundation would fund, and ultimately the foundation did begin to do so, in a relatively modest way. But the possibility of learning from these programs or interrelating them in some way with policy and research seemed impossible. There has always been a gap between people working on the ground and those doing research and writing in the academe. It is rare that such people learn from each other, although I have seen this kind of integration and collaboration attempted by some particularly imaginative women's groups. For example, AWARE, the Association of Women for Action and Research, located in Singapore, connects researchers, policy makers, and service providers, all working on issues having to do with domestic violence.

Valuing the Power of Caring and Commitment

It became increasingly clear to me as I traveled widely representing the Hewlett Foundation that money, though very helpful, was not what made an organization especially effective. The ingredient that provides life to an organization, as water does to a garden, is the commitment and drive of the people who are connected within the group. I have seen women, in the face of seemingly impossible conditions, working together, creating community, and helping others. On a trip in 2003 to Butula, in western Kenya, I asked a woman what kept her focused on the seemingly impossible task of preventing HIV/AIDS in her community. Her reply: "I believe that things can be better. I believe that I can make a difference to people. I am strengthened by working with and for others."

Of course money helps. But many women have told me that far more important than the money is the belief in their work, the sense that they are connected to a larger network of caring people, and the idea that no matter what the outcome, what they were doing made sense. Time and time again, I would arrive in a village, having come far over muddy roads in a jeep. I would listen and learn and be inspired and humbled by what women were doing, by their commitment and passion. I often felt like apologizing, saying, "I'm so sorry. I've interrupted you in your work." I felt that I was taking valuable time from them, but they would say, and I could see on their faces and in their actions, that they welcomed me there. They liked my asking questions. They appreciated that I was somebody from far, far away who cared about what they were doing. They wanted to hear what I thought. They wanted to know that we shared values. They wanted to feel connected with someone outside of their immediate surroundings; it strengthened them.

We are all empowered by connections from outside or far away, by support from somebody who may or may not even be like us but who sees us and positively acknowledges what we are doing. When we receive this support, we can go back to our work renewed. Over time, I grew to understand that this kind of connection, along with steady, unqualified support, was a critically important element for effecting change in the world. I became someone who approached people and places as a listener, seeking to learn and to give unqualified support and trust, rather than an expert, striving to teach or to tell others how to do things in a better way. I learned that caring and connecting were just as important as any money we could offer. I sought to echo Thich Nhat Hanh's mantra on love: "Dear One: I am here for you."[2]

In addition, I was becoming increasingly convinced of the nonmainstream notion that women were pivotal in all development work. At the same time, I was coming to the even less popular idea that we needed to support women's efforts in general, in trusting, unqualified ways, not just through groups created to address "women's issues" but through groups that were managed and governed by women. I didn't want to tie possible support for women to family planning or some other specific program area. I believed that our programs should be geared to leadership, community building, and empowerment in general.

The troubling disconnects in the Hewlett Foundation program persisted through the late 1970s and the early 1980s. The more villages and local programs I visited, the more I was struck by the fact that we were continuing to look at the issues of population and development in fragmented ways. We were not as successful as we wanted to be because we were not connecting important data points. What's more, a key element — the full participation of women — was not in the picture at all. This limited, ineffective, and wasteful approach to problems had to change.

I strongly felt that interrelating these seemingly different areas would help us help others — especially those who have been grossly neglected (women) — to take control of their own environments. Those environments are immediate (the body, the family, the household garden) or broader (the village, the state, the nation). Learning to control one's fertility can change a person's view of the wider world. Learning to plant trees (and space them wisely) can affect a person's view of the number of children she or he desires. Feeling more in control of one's life can lead a person to be more concerned about the environment and other development issues and to feel empowered to make choices about all sorts of things. *Everything is connected.* Instead of addressing issues of interest only to our donors and our board of directors, I felt our programs needed to be geared toward empowering the people who were at the center of population and development problems — women.

I visited villages and questioned myself about whether those of us in the grant-making world, sitting in California, Geneva, London, New York, Washington, and other cities, were truly effecting change with our multimillion-dollar budgets and our carefully devised programs. How much of the money that left our desks actually reached the people who needed it? Did any of it ever reach the women walking from their villages to share their thoughts and needs with other women? Did it make sense to continue doing our business as it had always been done when staring in my face was evidence that the people closest to the problems often had very different ideas? Clearly, it was time for me to move on, to get out of the world of large donors and find — or create — another organization.

As I neared the end of my ten years at the Hewlett Foundation, I found that my travels and increasing experience in the world of international development had raised nothing but questions and doubts about the ways that money was being given away around the world. I didn't have all of the answers to the questions that were pestering me, but I began to know that we could not possibly create fundamental change without connecting with, learning from, and listening to those women with their black bags in Nigeria, the village women in Nepal, and the groups of women in Mombasa — as well as the thousands of other women like them in villages, towns, and cities around the world.

Firmly convinced that enhancing the status of women was an essential part of all development efforts, particularly programs having to do with population and family planning, I began, as I mentioned earlier, to actively campaign for a women's program at the Hewlett Foundation. Ultimately, I failed in my attempt to institute such a program there. Nevertheless, not many years later, the idea that we need to empower women in all development efforts was brought to the center of international discussion at the United Nations International Conference on Population and Development, held in Cairo in 1994. We embodied this idea, too, within the programs of The Global Fund for Women, which, it turned out, was generously supported by members of the Hewlett family, who became solidly supportive of the concepts, programs, values, and style of The Global Fund.

As I have tried to describe, the tremendous opportunities that the Hewlett Foundation offered me, as well as the frustrations and obstacles that I encountered there, taught me a great deal about connection, among other things. And I was about to learn more about the power of passionate, like-minded people connecting around shared vision, goals, plans, and style.

In the course of creating The Global Fund for Women, I would make common cause with many people who wanted to address the roots of many problems — the basic inequalities in society, perpetuated through hierarchical social systems. We felt that addressing only the symptoms of these inequities was impractical, unfair, and dangerous because it demeaned 51 percent of the world's population.

What might happen, we wondered, if a small group of committed people (as small as three or five women, perhaps) or a foundation, or a fund, sought to form a web of connections among people, enabling women to enter and transform places previously closed to them by deliberate design or entrenched tradition? I was soon to find out.

Things to Remember
as You Cultivate Your Dreams

- People coming together in groups are a powerful force for social change.

- Include rather than exclude.

- Value diversity.

- Treat all in an evenhanded way.

- Connect rather than separate; integrate rather than fragment.

- Give generously and freely; provide flexible general support.

CHAPTER FOUR

Dream and Clarify
Your Vision

———— ∞∂∞∂∞∂ ————

Passion is a complicated word with many meanings. Its meanings include enduring suffering or being affected by something outside of ourselves, or strong emotions, or strong desires. It is a word that captures the spirit of our lives.... Our passion makes the best of us.

— From an Easter sermon, St. Marks Episcopal Church,
Palo Alto, California, 1998

As the idea for The Global Fund for Women became my passion, I was eager to move forward and felt as though nothing could stop me. I felt very much as Joshua Cooper Ramo described Steve Case, the founder of America Online, as someone with a dream for change: "Being a visionary is not the same thing as being popular. Odds are, if you're a visionary, most of your years have been a struggle to get others to see what is so apparent to you. This requires arguing people out of long-held beliefs, absorbing countless verbal assaults, and clinging to your judgment while friends wonder when you'll start explaining your position to your dog. Yet with every passing day, you grow more certain that you're right."[1]

My work over many years had led me to imagine something that to some people seemed an impossible dream: the creation of an international women's fund that would not only give away millions of dollars but would give this money in a way that was different — more flexible, more trusting — from the usual practices of foundations. I was sure that this was important — essential, really — and though I didn't know exactly how it could be done, the passion behind the dream fueled the hard work of finding out.

I don't exaggerate when I say I became a fanatic about The Fund, utterly driven from the evening when the idea kept me awake all night through the first four or five years of the life of the organization. Several people were excited by the idea of The Fund, and virtually everybody I spoke with about it seemed interested, but my enthusiasm went far beyond interest and excitement. I ate, drank, slept, and didn't sleep The Global Fund for Women. I was filled with passionate conviction. I was determined to do whatever it would take to make The Fund happen.

Without intending to detract from the previous chapter's discussion of connection or to downplay the important roles of countless other people in the early days of The Global Fund, I cite Paul Hawken's belief, stated in *Growing a Business*,[2] that start-up organizations generally succeed only when at least one person is willing to do anything to make them work. I was that person at The Global Fund for Women. You may well be that person in your own efforts to pursue a dream of change.

I was fanatical. I was dogmatic. I knew I was right! There is no doubt that this was a very annoying characteristic of me at the time, but I had no choice in the matter. (Everyone who crossed my path, including my cat, Max, knew all about The Global Fund for Women!) When I asked one man for a ten thousand dollar donation, he said, "Anne, surely there are other ways to save the world. You speak as if empowering women is the only intervention that will make such positive change. Do you really believe that this is the key intervention?" Without a moment's hesitation, I answered, "Yes." I had known this man for a while, so I guess he knew that at base I wasn't a dogmatic, crazed person. He made the donation, becoming one of our founding donors, though I know that he thought that my views were extreme. But that opinion didn't matter to me; I was driven.

There's a vulnerability in this kind of unquestioning drive; you have to be willing to look like, and perhaps even be, an extremist. If you aren't willing to do that, then others who might have joined in the vision may hold back, which could diminish the chances of your vision coming to fruition.

Nothing quite like our vision for The Global Fund existed in the world of philanthropy. Daring to dream such a grand — some might, and did, say grandiose — dream is not unrealistic, even if the dream is never fully realized. Such a goal motivates, inspires, and becomes a renewable source of energy. Never mind if people suggest that you are "unrealistically idealistic." That can be a good thing. Major change seldom occurs without such "unrealistic" idealism. Your dream also acts to galvanize others. My dream of getting money directly into the hands of women on the ground in respectful, trusting, and flexible ways inspired a good number of people on that founding weekend and in the months and years to come. Let yourself dream.

Turning Vision into Something Real

Vision is fuel, energy, passion — or, as I like to suggest, as important as water to a garden. Unless that vision is clear in your mind, it is hard, if not impossible, to complete the process of refining your dream into an actionable plan. Furthermore, without clarity of vision the hard work and pain that come with setting in place a program or organization become all the more intense, as I would learn during the formative stage of The Global Fund.

To be sure, our dream was big, but it was not vague. This is important. Years of experience and learning had shown me how to avoid bad program practices and had given me a strong sense of what I should try instead. I wanted this new organization to:

- respond to rather than set agendas;

- respect small efforts, knowing that bigger isn't necessarily better;

- eschew bureaucracy and rigid hierarchy; and

- always listen and learn.

The clarity and coherence of your vision and plans for change are basic to establishing goals, setting up administrative and financial procedures, hiring appropriate staff people, developing program and fund-raising plans, and creating the very structure that allows your vision to become reality. Most important, clarity of vision is appealing to others, allowing them to understand and support this dream of change.

In the beginning, during the weekend at the conference in Philadelphia, my vision was pretty simple: I wanted to set up a foundation that would make money available to women to carry out programs defined, planned, and managed by women rather than suggested by and/or directed by donors. As I spoke with friends and colleagues at the conference and in the weeks following it, again and again I was asked, "How can I help?" Three women whom I had known through my foundation work offered money (five thousand dollars each), and I asked them if they would become a founding donor committee. (I made up the idea of a group of "founding donors" on the spot.)

Soon after that fateful weekend, when I was back home in California, Lynn Marsh, a friend and graphic artist, who had patiently listened to my endless talk about the new organization, asked what she could do to help. I immediately asked if she could design a letterhead, in case we might receive and write some letters. (No email in those days, remember!) She then asked a couple of very obvious questions: "What is the actual name of this organization?" and "What address should we put on the letterhead?" Hmmm. Good questions!

We hadn't decided on a name, and we certainly didn't have an address. But I learned, if only from one of my grandchildren's books, *Riding Freedom* by Pam Muñoz Ryan,[3] that "Naming something's important.... A name should stand for something." Businesses of various kinds spend vast amounts of time and money researching, convening focus groups, and testing names for products and brands. Names and the other words (slogans, mission statements, ads, et cetera) that create the identity for your organization are vitally important. They need to embody your dream and passion. People completely unfamiliar with your idea should hear the phrase and either get it immediately or be intrigued enough to figure it out. Some names are perfectly clear. For example, the International Business Machines Corporation, now known as IBM, was named for the products it sells. But other names are just intriguing. In the cases of Apple Computer and MoveOn.org, for example, the meanings aren't particularly clear, but an apple is nice, simple, and healthy, something that everyone might want to have at home, and to "move on" suggests progress toward the future.

When you ask people for money or other kinds of support, they need to feel good about aligning themselves with you and your organization — and they are likely to look first at the way the name of your group represents its work in the world. Since the name is this important, you might wonder if it is necessary to hire professionals or to possess special advertising or marketing skills in order to coin a winning name or phrase for your effort or group. In my view, it is not.

At the conference in Philadelphia, I played around with various ways of describing the women's fund idea; I alternately called it an international foundation for women, a women's international fund, a fund for women, and a global fund. After speaking with my artist friend, I asked the other three founding board members — Dame Nita Barrow, Frances Kissling, and Laura Lederer — to indicate their favorite from among a list of names or to provide me with more ideas. The possible names I presented to them were: the International Foundation for Women, the Women's International Fund, the Global Foundation for Women, the Women's Global Fund, and The Global Fund for Women. After a phone call or two, we unanimously chose The Global Fund for Women. Frances made the specific point that the name should be The Global Fund for Women — with a capital T — and we followed that good idea from the beginning. In a few short and memorable words, this name captured the idea and embodied the vision: a pool of money that would be available for women globally. Capitalizing the T in

The also made the group something very special from that small beginning. As usual, a group of a few women worked wonders!

Lynn, my artist friend, was delighted. She said, "I am so glad that you used *global* rather than *international*; *global* is rounder, fuller, more female-seeming."

And, she reminded me, what about the address? I did not want to use my home address, striving from the outset to have the organization be an entity unto itself rather than being directly associated with a founder. I did not want to use a post office box either, because to me "P.O. box" brings to mind something tiny. Though our organization was very young, it really was very big. I couldn't imagine fitting it into a post office box.

Racking my brain for a possible address, I thought of another friend, Cole Wilbur, the executive director of the David and Lucile Packard Foundation, who had been very supportive of the idea of a women's global fund at the conference in Philadelphia. I remember calling his office on a Sunday, a few days after returning from Philadelphia, thinking that I would leave a message on his office machine. Instead, the phone was picked up, and it was Cole, working through the weekend. He suggested I meet him at his office that afternoon to discuss the new fund. In our meeting, I asked if we could place a small box in the Packard Foundation office, where mail could collect (if anyone were to write to us) and I could pick it up occasionally. He not only agreed that we could use the Packard Foundation address; he asked if we needed an office space, since the foundation had just moved into a new building and had some empty offices to spare. This was tremendously exciting. All of a sudden, we had not only an address but also a room of our own!

While we were in such a positive mood, I asked him if it

might be possible for the Packard Foundation to consider offer-ing a grant to The Fund, now that we were beginning to actually set up the organization. This required a proposal, which Laura and I wrote up quite quickly. Because we did not yet have our IRS 501(c)(3) status (a necessary regulatory step in order to qual-ify as a not-for-profit organization and to receive tax-deductible dollars in the United States), the Packard Foundation people not only approved the grant, they also agreed to serve as our fiscal agent for a short time.

An additional generous touch from the Packard Foundation was a phone call the next day from a lovely woman there who was responsible for arranging for office furniture. "Do you need any-thing?" she asked. Little did she know that we needed everything, but I said that a couple of desks and chairs and maybe a file cab-inet or two would be wonderful.

As I think of this time, of the excitement of the idea and the generosity of people, I think of a conversation I had years later with a group of women in Zimbabwe when I visited there in 1992. They told me about an idea they had for a women's center; they wanted to create a place where women could come together and meet and where documentation about the women's situa-tion in Zimbabwe would have a home. I urged them to apply to The Global Fund for Women for a small grant. This they did, and it was the beginning of the Zimbabwe Women's Resource Centre and Network. Some years afterward, the women told me that even though they had had a dream of a women's center and even though they had written a short proposal to obtain a grant, it was when they were told that the grant was forthcoming that they looked at each other and said, "Well, now I guess we have to do it! We have to do what we have dreamed of and what we have written about!" It was then that they began to talk with friends about finding an office, hiring a part-time worker, getting a telephone installed, and beginning work. Support from the outside was not essential, surely, but it helped a great deal.

So it was with us. When those three women donors at the conference offered money, when the Packard Foundation offered a place, with space and furniture, when Apple Computer responded positively to our request for a computer and printer (which happened very soon after the office gift), I realized that we no longer only had a dream; we now had to make very specific plans about how to build the organization that would be the vehicle for the dream.

I mention these seemingly minor administrative events in some detail for a number of reasons. First, turning your dream into reality requires all sorts of little tasks, some of them quite unanticipated. Second, you can take care of these many tasks quite smoothly; if your vision is clear, things fall into place. Clarity of vision and passionate determination can create the kind of getting-things-done and getting-support domino effect that we experienced at the beginning of The Fund. Have I mentioned yet that we were also having fun?

Sharing the Vision and Receiving Help

Our early success getting people to share our vision for The Global Fund was actually a lesson in fund-raising and leadership. Sharing the idea and getting immediate and very positive feedback was exciting and empowering. The feedback strengthened me to ask for more help. It confirmed my belief in the basic generosity of people. When we passionately presented the idea to other women and men and it made sense to them, they joined in with ideas, excitement, and support. It is true that in order to receive, one has to ask. But everything depends on the vision — the clarity of vision.

As you inspire with your vision, you will be inspired in turn. One such moment occurred very soon after The Global Fund's inception, during a board meeting of Women and Foundations/Corporate Philanthropy (now called Women and Philanthropy), a group that works to encourage greater participation by women in the philanthropic world. We board members went around a circle in a sort of round-robin, bringing everyone up to date on our activities. One of the few men on that board, Tom Layton, announced that he wanted to give me his allotted time in order to hear more about ideas for The Global Fund for Women. The discussion lasted for a few minutes, and then he took out his checkbook and wrote a check to The Global Fund for one hundred dollars. He wanted to be the first individual donor (after the founders) to The Global Fund for Women because he thought the idea was so important. The clarity of our vision inspired his action, and his action, in turn, inspired and empowered me. It also reminded me, yet again, of the power that comes through simple acts of generosity and kindness.

For the most part, those first few months reinforced the initial vision. Many individual donors supported the idea, among them some thirty people who became founding donors by dint of pledging at least five thousand dollars over the first eighteen months. Our plan was to give away money — a task I knew something about. But to give away money, you have to raise it. The early weeks and months were so encouraging that I somehow thought the idea of The Fund was so good that lots of people would just write checks and we would raise millions of dollars in very short order. I had a great deal to learn, as it turned out, and we will discuss this in detail in chapter 8.

Creating Processes and Structures
Consistent with the Vision

Our challenge at The Global Fund was to give money away while also encouraging the empowerment of grant recipients. Given the power of money in some societies, including the United States, being in the twofold business of money and empowerment presented a challenge. Was it possible to give away money in such a way that the process would not disempower the recipients? Empowerment of others was central to our vision. Making that vision a reality in the world, in our day-to-day operations, entailed developing processes and structures that strengthened relationships, created trust, encouraged freedom, and generally added value far beyond the money that was given away. This meant creating a style of operating that was itself empowering.

During the many years I had spent working in the foundation world, I had seen several program officers in foundations disempower people in the process of grant-making because the officers believed that they knew more about program design and implementation than the people to whom they were granting money. I had seen arrogance in the foundation world, arrogance that played upon differing power relationships among people, especially with regard to money. Some program officers even acted as if the money was *theirs* to give away.

At The Global Fund, I was determined that there was not going to be such behavior. But in practical terms, what did this mean? What processes and structures would ensure that we would not undermine or disempower the very groups that we wanted to work with, given the issue of money and power?

The answers to these questions revealed themselves over the first several years of the life of The Global Fund as we developed the style of The Fund, and we will look at them more closely in the chapters to come. During the early stage of The Fund, however, our intention of promoting empowerment meant such actions as deciding that we would receive proposals in any language (this required our setting in place a network of volunteer translators and establishing a connection with the Monterey School of Languages). It meant not second-guessing grantees about what they thought was important to them and instead fully respecting their definitions of their own needs and the solutions to their problems. It meant actively listening and learning from others always. It meant looking at each proposal in an evenhanded way with real curiosity. It meant understanding that money is not the key driving force behind real change.

As you begin to build the structures and processes of your program or organization, it is important to continually revisit what you are trying to accomplish. What is the problem that you are addressing, that you are trying to solve? What is your vision for change? Are you concerned about how people treat each other? Are you concerned about inequality and injustice? Make sure that your processes and structures are in sync with your vision for change. Your structures, therefore, will be fair, generous, and respectful; staff members and others who are part of your program will treat each other with respect and kindness; and so on. The way you do your work can be transformative. The medium is the message.

Although our organization was conceived to be different from others in the philanthropic world, I would hesitate to say that it was unique. There were very good program officers in the foundation world, working respectfully with grantees. There were women's funds working with groups in the United States, and there were international organizations working to make positive change for women through various programs. As you work to clarify your vision and to translate it into practical terms, should you be concerned about being unique, the first, or in some way groundbreaking? Not really. The program or organization will be unique simply because you are building it, you are leading it. As Martha Graham said, "There is only one of you in all time," and if you don't take action, "the world will not have it."[4]

In my case, The Global Fund was the organization that I could be deeply passionate about because it was the one where I could perhaps establish some control over the style of our work as well as *what* we did. Integrating the what and the *how* was important to me personally. I wanted to do good work in my life, and I wanted to feel good about doing the work every day. This was a matter of coherence and integration for me.

If you feel that your dream for change is unique, then your heart and passion will be in it and you can inspire others to join you. But the fact that other organizations or programs with similar intentions may exist or that other organizations may be addressing similar problems are not reasons to be concerned or to limit your own dreams and plans. There are plenty of problems that need to be addressed in various ways. There is plenty of work for all of us.

Responding Constructively to Negative Feedback

Most of the people to whom I preached the gospel of The Global Fund for Women with my early, missionary-like zeal responded with enthusiasm and offers of help. But there were a few — among them some people I greatly respected — who said, "You can't do it. You'll never raise the money." Some asked, "How will you locate groups without sending staff overseas?" Or, "Where are the donors? Where will you get the money?" After all, we were creating The Global Fund for Women precisely because there was so little money for women's organizations internationally. Was the money really there? Some naysayers believed that it would be impossible to raise the money without the central involvement of one or two very wealthy women. Others told me that I wouldn't be able to create an accountable organization that gave away money on a worldwide basis by depending on volunteers in the countries involved.

A few months into the creation of The Global Fund, we reached out to some of the people working on domestic and international women's issues, notably at the United Nations Development Fund for Women (UNIFEM) and at some of the U.S.-based women's foundations. When we shared our ideas about developing The Global Fund for Women, the immediate response from several groups was, "Why create another organization? We're already doing that work." I tried to explain that we hoped to work collaboratively with other groups, that we planned to support small organizations directly rather than working through overseas offices and through government partners, as UNIFEM, for example, did. The fact that we could work independently, I argued, would mean that we could support groups working on more controversial issues than could an official agency of the United Nations.

Among those who questioned the creation of a new group was the president of one of the women's funds. When I explained that we were going to work outside the United States, whereas her organization was U.S.-based, she said, "But we are thinking of moving to the international." My response was that there was plenty of work for all, and, indeed, over the years, we all have been able to collaborate successfully, defining our own individual parts of the large set of problems that characterize the world, especially for women. In addition, we invited women from these sister organizations to serve on our advisory council. As you build your program or organization, you will want to learn from and draw in others who are working on similar issues, especially those who may at first seem unsupportive of your ideas and your new program.

Some people may feel threatened by a new organization because they think that it will drain off some of the funds that might otherwise go to their existing organizations. Although such feelings may be understandable, my experience has led me to believe that there is not some limited amount of money that gets divided up, like a pie. I believe that creating new groups that bring different perspectives and that are well run can only result in the pie growing larger. More money pours into a field when more people enter it and make donors aware of the problems and the needs. This is what seemed to happen in the case of The Global Fund and international women's issues.

❦

In a roundabout way over time, negative feedback can help clarify one's vision and plans. Initially, though, such comments shook my faith just a little, and I allowed myself to consider the possibility that these people could be right. Was it too great a risk to start an organization from scratch, without much idea of where the money was going to come from? Maybe. On the other hand, in my work in international philanthropy, I had seen firsthand that women were unfairly treated with regard to financial and other resources, and I knew there were people who cared about such inequality and who might support the endeavor. Critics and pessimists forced me to reexamine my assumptions and plans — not a bad thing.

But the criticism did worry me. A little doubt crept into my consciousness, and that was not good; I needed all the energy I could get, and doubt can sap energy. So, during one of our frequent phone calls, I talked with Frances about it. After I recounted the negative conversations, she gave me some excellent advice. Essentially, she advised me to stop listening to negative ideas and negative people. That's not what I needed at that moment. She was so right! When you are putting together a new organization or program, like a newly planted garden, it is fragile, and you need positive responses and nurturing. If you are determined to create the new program or organization, you may listen to negative feedback, but you must transform it as soon as possible into constructive action. In the early days of an organization, keep the vision clear, get on with your plans, open yourself to helpful suggestions — and avoid negative people.

The naysayers had raised some useful questions: How were we going to raise the money? How was I going to deal with my belief that we could realize our dreams without depending on one or two very wealthy people? How were we going to ensure our accountability without locating staff around the world? Ultimately, we figured out how to deal with these valid questions, but in the meantime, I did not allow myself to believe that it could not be done. Instead, the question simply became, How will we do this, in the context of our dreams and beliefs? I learned that at the beginning it was both wise and strategic to hold the new creation lovingly and put it in the care of others who loved it too.

We who loved it could hypothesize answers for only so long; at this point, it seemed timely to seek ideas and help from people outside the inner circle of Fund founders and friends, so we decided to have two meetings — one, a small meeting of about eight members of the inner circle, people who knew about and were committed to our vision; and the second, a meeting of about twenty people from organizations working internationally on women's issues.

Out of these meetings, held in early 1988, came clearer ideas for programs. There was an overarching interest in female human rights. There was also interest in women's access to communications and particularly modern communications technology, in women's economic autonomy, and in education of the philanthropic community about international women's work. We listened carefully to colleagues who took the time to share their opinions about what was needed, and we began to develop a program that we could clearly and compellingly describe in our first brochure. Like deciding upon a name, putting these early words on paper, either for an informational brochure or for a proposal, is crucial to your own clarity of thought and to the process of presenting your vision to the world.

Moving from Being the Volunteer to Being the Paid Leader

Toward the end of 1987 — six months into the life of The Global Fund — we had learned a great deal, we had produced a descriptive brochure, and we seemed quite clear about what we dreamed of doing and why. In other words, we had a clear vision. Now came the practical matters of creating the structures and processes to carry through with our vision. In the chapters to follow, I discuss a variety of these matters. But I touch on them here, before moving to other discussions, to illustrate the central importance of leadership.

By the end of the first eighteen months of the life of The

Fund, I had hired a part-time office manager/secretary. Meanwhile, I and other volunteers — primary among them Frances — raised money, prepared for board meetings, dealt with lawyers, and so on. All of us were doing this on the side, while we worked elsewhere for pay. In my case, I was finishing up my ten years with the Hewlett Foundation and later teaching at the University of California, San Francisco, School of Medicine. I would go into The Fund office when I could, at least every weekend, and I talked often with our office manager, who worked a few hours a week. We had raised about $150,000 by the end of 1987, mostly from men and women who joined our list of founding donors.

By June 1988, it had become obvious that we had to go beyond our part-time paid help and our volunteer leadership. So much was happening as The Global Fund kept growing, and we clearly needed a paid, full-time executive to run the organization. When the little board of friends, meeting in my living room, urged me to drop my other work and become the full-time staff director of The Global Fund by January 1989, I half panicked. I agreed in principle, but in my mind I was not committed to the idea.

Could I, should I risk taking on the job of running an organization and raising the money for my own salary? I was afraid to give up my teaching and consulting. We had raised enough money to run the organization for only three months and give some grants. But my salary, if there were to be one, would have to drop drastically. I was fifty-two years old, and surely the move would be unwise financially. I had been thinking about my old age and feeling a little vulnerable, to the point of identifying with bag ladies and homeless women, as almost every woman I know does at some stage in her life. In other words taking on the job of paid (rather than volunteer) executive filled me with anxiety.

I was also concerned about how my leadership would alter the dynamics of the group. At that point, the board consisted of six people. Although we had our differences, we were equal and united in our vision and caring for the organization. I knew that if I became the paid leader, my relationships with the other founders and board members would change. I had a vague idea of an organization that could operate with little or no hierarchy, but I knew in my gut that if I took on the job of executive, I would become "staff" and it would be hard to maintain equality. I liked the relationships we had, and I didn't want them to change. So I continued to mull over whether I would take the job or whether we should advertise for and hire someone else to manage the organization with our direction.

By October 1988, I had to make a final decision about whether I would take on the job of running The Global Fund on a paid basis. As I considered this question, I decided to take off a Saturday morning to clean up my garage and prune some trees, and I began by picking up a huge pile of papers to recycle. As I stepped out of my front door, I tripped over the doorstep, fell, and felt and heard a crack in my right foot. After a phone call to my friend Barry and a trip to the urgent care center, I found myself on crutches, with a broken foot that had to be kept up for at least two or three weeks. All of a sudden, I had plenty of time to sit still and think about what I truly wanted to do.

Neither Barry nor my daughter could understand my hesitation. They both knew that my heart and spirit were completely invested in creating The Global Fund for Women. I knew that too, but I was afraid to take the risk of being without a predictable income, let alone some money for my older age. And yet, I knew that it would be impossible to realize my vision without devoting my full time to it. Could I raise the money? Was it possible? Raising money to give to women overseas through grants was quite possible, of course. But raising money for my own salary and the salaries of others? Could I and should I try?

Resting for a while, having other people bring me cups of tea, and just taking time to clarify my ideas made the decision easy in the end. I really didn't have a choice. I had to bring my vision to fruition. I was driven, and I decided to follow my dream — to work full-time toward creating a worldwide women's fund that would give away millions of dollars to women's groups so that women would come into full equality and full participation in the world.

In January 1989, I officially took over as the paid, full-time executive of The Global Fund for Women. My title was president and chief executive officer. I stepped down as chair of the board, and one of the other six members moved into that position. As time would tell, I had been right that some of the relationships were destined to change.

Having made the leap to take on the responsibility of running the organization on a nonvoluntary basis, I became excited. I was determined to build an organization based on the principles that I hold dear. I had not forgotten the women with their mopeds and their black bags — their caring, their humor, their trust, and their visions for positive change. I had not forgotten what they had taught me about community, inclusion, evenhandedness, and generosity of spirit. My memories of their strength and their hope for change strengthened me.

Your initial dream, along with the real world testing you to turn your dream into a clear plan of action, will strengthen you as well as your effort.

Things to Remember
as You Cultivate Your Dreams

- Dare to dream of positive change.

- Clarify your dream, your vision. Be as clear as possible about what you hope to do and why.

- Share your vision and plans with others who are working in the same field. Seek their advice and counsel. Learn from them. Draw them in.

- Be optimistic and avoid naysayers in the early years. Turn pessimistic thoughts into "to do" lists.

- Know that to give reality to your vision, the leadership required of you will involve a lot of work and may change relationships with others.

- Recall these words of Helen Adams Keller: "Security is mostly a superstition.... Life is either a daring adventure or nothing at all."[5] Take the risk!

CHAPTER FIVE

Practice Your Principles
to Avoid Confusion

There is no reason why good cannot triumph as often as evil.
The triumph of anything is a matter of organization. If there
are such things as angels, hope that they are organized along
the lines of the Mafia.

— Kurt Vonnegut, Jr.

One day when I was giving a talk at Stanford on the situation of women around the world and on the accomplishments of the many groups of women globally who were addressing those issues, I fielded various questions about the work of The Global Fund and especially the need for fairness and justice for women. One question was like none I had encountered before. A woman stood up and asked, "Do you believe in good and evil? Do you see your work in these terms?" To be honest, I had never really thought of the work of The Global Fund in that way, probably because I had avoided seeing things as *either/or* and because I don't like conceiving of relationships as adversarial. However, the questioner set me thinking, as did the Vonnegut quote above when I came across it.

There were times when it was tempting to consider that evil influences were at work, as we responded to women facing issues such as bride burning, genital mutilation, honor killings, rape, persistent pay inequity, and so on. The women addressing these issues were, in our view, truly good, and we tried to do good too as we supported them in their struggles to make positive change. But no matter whether one really believes in the presence of evil or aspires to be an angel, there is no question that one needs to be well organized in order to do good effectively.

Being well organized can mean a lot of things, starting with knowing both why you are doing what you are doing and how you plan to do it. To be organized, one needs vision, a mission, an action plan, and, I believe, a clear set of principles to guide the work. Although the vision, mission, and guiding principles of The Fund developed and were modified over the years, we set them out in simple terms in the very beginning, in the first annual report, which covered the first two fiscal years, July 1987 to June 1989. We described the vision in various ways in a couple of essays; basically, it came down to our hope for "justice and dignity for all life on earth."

The mission was much clearer. We stated it thus:

- To provide funds to seed, strengthen, and link groups that are committed to women's well-being and that work for their full participation in society

- To encourage increased support for women's programs globally

- To provide leadership in promoting a greater understanding of the importance of supporting women's full
  participation internationally

After you have developed some ideas about your mission
(essentially a statement about what problems you are trying to
solve or what issues you are trying to address), the next step is
to lay out a program that will describe the direction that you
intend to take as you work toward accomplishing the mission.
I am reminded here of a statement by David Packard, after he
had written the short book *The HP Way* on how he and Bill
Hewlett had built the Hewlett-Packard Company: "You've got
to have leadership, you've got to know what you're doing, and
you've got to play it straight."[1] In my terms, he was referring
to clarity of vision (a key component of leadership), organization (knowing what you are doing), and principles (playing it
straight).

Developing Guiding Principles

A vitally important step in being organized is to develop a set of
principles that will guide your work. Clear principles allow for
easier management and governance and result in a style that can
characterize an organization.

At The Global Fund, we noted in our annual reports our commitment to giving flexible, timely support to women's groups
working on emerging, controversial, or difficult issues. We further stated that our programs were expressions of a set of values
at the base of the creation of The Fund that had been affirmed
by The Fund's board of directors as themes that would characterize our programs. These developed into the following guiding

principles, which we published in all of our annual reports during the first nine years:

- We value and respect the wisdom and experience of women in all their diversity.

- We believe that women themselves know best how to determine their needs.

- We believe that an equal partnership between women and men is critical to furthering global well-being, and we recognize the current imbalance in this relationship.

- We believe that women working together is an effective way of helping women achieve their fair and rightful place in the world.

- We believe that an organization's structures and processes should reflect its principles.

Related to these beliefs were other concepts — such as evenhandedness, generosity, compassion, trust, openness, and learning — which we also expressed throughout our annual reports. Notice that we were concerned primarily with how we were going to do our work; we envisioned processes emerging over time and being governed by these principles.

Every day in our decisions and actions we consciously tried to live by these principles and values, to apply our beliefs in diversity and integration rather than separation, transparency and openness rather than secrecy, evenhandedness rather than favoritism, curiosity and learning rather than arrogance, inclusion rather than exclusion, and trust rather than suspicion. I began to see our efforts as an attempt to work within a very different paradigm from the one we saw around us in the United States in the 1990s.

Although we certainly took time at board and staff meetings to talk about these concepts and note how we were trying to apply them, we didn't engage in endless meetings to develop them. Our early ideas about what we would do and how we would do it were embodied in grant proposals — the one we wrote for the Packard Foundation and another, a year later, that we submitted to the Ford Foundation. These proposals, which became the templates for all of our later grant proposals, were essentially business plans. At first, it was the cofounders who defined what we were hoping to do and how we would do it. Later, when we all decided to revisit the list of values and principles, another person on the board took on the job of rewriting them and gathering the reactions of board and staff members. She continued to lead the effort to clarify these concepts as both our staff and our board agreed upon them.

During one of these reviews, a young staff person, Mila Visser 't Hooft, suggested that we formally add to our list of guiding principles the very important value that "an organization's structures and processes should reflect its principles." I latched on to this idea immediately, believing that organizations should strive to be models of how we want the world and our relationships to be. This "new" guiding principle was added to our list at The Fund, and since then, on every board on which I have served I have suggested that we add and live by this stated and clear belief.

Putting Your Principles in Print

We published our guiding beliefs and principles because we thought that it was important to be clear and public about what we believed. I strongly encourage you to do the same. List these items in your annual report, in proposals, on websites, and in mailings. Doing this allows for clarity in your own mind and offers guidance to staff and others associated with the program or organization. Of course the list can be modified over time as it becomes evident that some of these beliefs are more fundamental to the style of your organization and its staff and board than are others.

Not everyone thinks that making principles clear and public is particularly important. For example, I once spoke with a consultant who had been hired to develop the guiding principles of an organization created to provide a network for international nongovernmental organizations (NGOs). He informed me that "Everyone understands the principles; there is no need to publish them. We all know that an organization should live by its principles." I, on the contrary, believe it *is* important to make known one's principles and values and to state them in public. They serve as guidelines for staff and board members, and they provide bases for discussions about how to develop programs in consistent ways. Also, when conflicts or confusions crop up you can return to the published principles for guidance. For example, if diversity is among the principles, regularly question whether the board and staff are truly diverse. If not, take specific action to increase diversity. Or, if you are wondering whether to approve a grant or a program suggested by a group, and if you affirm the principle that people themselves know their needs best, then you can make your decision based on the answers to questions like these: Is the program a true reflection of the needs of the people being affected? Are they represented in the decision-making structure?

From decisions based on an organization's principles emerge structures and processes that embody those principles. Few organizations are able to truly live their principles in every circumstance, but stating them clearly, in writing, is a first step toward that ideal.

Being Accountable

Once you have presented your principles to the world, an important question soon arises: To whom are we accountable for fulfilling the mission and living up to the principles and values? In the case of The Global Fund, this question had many parts: Were we accountable to our donors? Were we accountable to the U.S. government (because of our nonprofit status)? Were we accountable to all women around the world, including the multitude of women who did not directly receive funding from us? Were we accountable to all of these groups of people?

We required grantee groups to be accountable for the use of the funds we granted to them, and we required reports from them. Applying the principle of evenhandedness, therefore, we ourselves needed to be accountable, certainly to our own donors as well as to the government (as a nonprofit organization governed by the regulations of the U.S. Internal Revenue Service). But were there others to whom we were obliged to account? As I thought about this issue, I concluded that we were accountable to many and therefore, in order to respond to this need for accountability, our work had to be characterized by openness and transparency; so these became guiding principles too. Therefore, in practice, we made it clear that our processes and structures were open to review by the world; anyone who wanted information about them could have it.

Every organization, whether for-profit or not-for-profit, needs to hold itself accountable by regularly reviewing whether its activities are serving the stakeholders, whether its programs are in alignment with its principles and vision, and whether its work is still relevant as times and external forces change.

Establishing a Team-Based Organizational Structure

Over time at The Fund, we developed structures and ways of operating that reflected our principles. Although we used some aspects of hierarchical systems, we consciously tried to create an organizational form that would stress participation, teamwork, and consultation. In an organization with a traditional, hierarchical structure, the organizational chart might look like a pyramid, with one or a few people at the top and many other people below. In an organization whose structure is geared more toward teamwork, the organizational chart may look more like a web or a network of interrelating loci of responsibility. This second type was more our style, with board, staff, advisors, donors, and grantees all operating in their own spheres of responsibility and interacting with each other openly and respectfully.

We recognized that we needed to have someone who would take responsibility for the day-to-day operations of the whole organization, and we knew that we had to give that person freedom to be creative and responsible. Although I was eager to move away from hierarchy, my experience suggested that an organization needs one person who will take ultimate responsibility for the health of the organization. At the same time, we knew we needed a board of directors, which we hoped would be a council of wise women, who with commitment and caring could monitor the work of the organization. I conceived of the board as a supporting partner in the organization, and I saw the staff as the experts in the day-to-day running of the organization, not that these ideas always worked out in practice. (Board and staff issues are further discussed in chapter 7.)

In the first years of The Global Fund, we all did a little of everything, with individual people taking responsibility for certain aspects of the program. Over the years, the staff grew, and responsibilities for grant-making, fund-raising, outreach, and administration became more specific. We began to develop teams, each led by one or two of the staff people, around the functional program areas of grant-making, fund-raising, and administration. As the leader of the organization itself, I served on all teams and was asked to carry out various responsibilities. Teams embodied The Fund's belief that people "working together is an effective way of helping women achieve their fair and rightful place in the world."

The team approach served a number of purposes, in addition to being in line with our principles. It spread the work across the desks of many people, giving staff members greater understanding of the work of the entire staff and enabling them to fill in somewhere beyond their specific jobs. It reduced hierarchy, since teams might be led by any one of the team members, and it resulted in a greater sense of community and individual empowerment. Most important, it gave individual staff members opportunities to lead — to articulate a goal for a task, to plan to reach that goal, and to involve others in the activity.

In one example of this practice, our youngest staff member coordinated all of the tasks related to our fund-raising mailings. It was her job to plan the mailings and make sure everything happened so the mailings were effective and got out on time. She let me know when it was time to write a fund-raising letter, gave me some ideas for that letter, and gave me a deadline by which to finish the letter and get it back to her. She also ordered all necessary supplies and organized the groups of volunteers who would come to fold the letters and stuff them into envelopes. (Incidentally, these volunteer days were great fun, with refreshments and lots of conviviality.) Throughout this whole process, she called upon certain staff members to review materials and plans and undertake specific tasks. She coordinated the team, and she took ultimate responsibility for meeting the goals for those activities.

Striving to Foster and Embody Diversity

Diversity is a principle that most organizations now would hope to embody, given our increasingly interdependent and multicultural world. At The Global Fund, we were committed to diversity from the beginning for the very obvious reason that we were working with women of all kinds from all around the world, and we wanted the organization to reflect that basic fact. We worked hard to diversify every part of our organization, following the principle of valuing and respecting "the wisdom and experience of women in all their diversity." But we were committed to maintaining diversity also because we believed the presence of many different perspectives led to excellence. So, we tried to diversify in many different ways — by nationality, ethnicity, race, age, sexual preference, et cetera.

By the third and fourth years, our small staff included a Latina woman, a South Asian woman, two non-American white women, a Vietnamese woman, a lesbian, a bisexual woman, and one white American woman. The board was quite diverse, about equally divided between U.S.-based and non-U.S.-based members, with good regional representation from around the world.

One woman on our staff became our window into the world of the disabled and inspired us with her growing strength and empowerment; another opened our eyes to the lives of immigrant families and courageous refugee experiences; and a third educated us on what it was like to be a lesbian in a heterosexual society. Diversity strengthened us, taught us a great deal, and resulted in a lively and delightful office atmosphere.

This is not to say that maintaining and thriving in a diverse environment was easy. The addition of every new board and staff member required some adjustment in the culture of the organization. We had to constantly create an atmosphere of trust and openness, so that new members would feel welcomed rather than marginalized, so they would be comfortable enough to speak up and participate rather than hold back. Here, once again, a culture of conscious learning was extremely helpful. Openness and the desire to learn have to be real; if they are, people with diverse backgrounds can work well together.

Frankly, though, sometimes maintaining such an environment was a pain. I remember thinking, as we added yet another board member with yet another very different perspective, what a burden it was to have to listen to truly intelligent people present challenging and even confrontational views. We had differences in priority, in the nature of our community, and in the ways in which we felt comfortable interacting. Sometimes I just felt like getting on with my own plans and ideas. But this variety of views made our meetings lively and intense, and we did not differ in our view of the basic mission of the organization or in our vision of empowerment and change for women.

Over the years, we made some mistakes. We failed to truly diversify our donor base, except to the extent that we obtained money from many different kinds of sources — individuals, foundations, corporations, various agencies, and so on. We would have preferred greater diversity within these categories, particularly among individual donors. Also, on one or two occasions, we added people to our board who were not able to put the good of the organization above their own personal agendas and needs. Such a situation is unacceptable in a healthy organization, and we had to find ways, mostly having to do with honesty and openness, to gracefully move such people off the board.

In one instance, we had a part-time staff person who brought with her not only some of the experience of belonging to at least two marginalized groups but also the anger and lack of trust that sometimes result from such marginalization. Her tenure with The Global Fund was brief because she chose to move on to another organization quite soon, but her influence lived on. We were concerned that there had been such difficulty integrating this person into our group, and we met more than once to express our thoughts and share our feelings about the situation. The staff decided that all of us would spend two days at a weekend workshop on diversity, in an effort to learn even more about listening and learning.

Our conscious attempt to understand, if not truly walk in the shoes of, the "other" seemed to me centrally and critically important to the success of our work. After all, we were in the business of spanning differences, crossing cultures, and interacting with people very different from ourselves on very sensitive issues. Until my time at The Global Fund, I had conceived of diversity as an honest attempt to understand another's point of view. The years at The Global Fund brought me to a belief that it was necessary and perhaps possible to go further than that, to try to become the other, to walk in her shoes, so to speak. I grew to realize that we had to make a conscious choice to be completely open and to learn and trust. Perhaps the kind of openness and trust that I am talking about is love. Whatever it is, such an approach to difference can bring about personal and perhaps even global transformation.

As I ponder the subject of diversity, I recall a day I spent with someone who on the surface could not have been more different from me, unless she had been a man. She was one of ten children who had grown up in a poor family in a village in southern Uganda. We took a couple of hours off from a conference because she was visiting the San Francisco Bay Area for the first time. I drove her up and down the hills of the city, across the Golden Gate Bridge, and out to the sea. We talked nonstop, finding that we were as one on every issue. Her father was a local village teacher who had encouraged her to go to high school, to college, and ultimately to graduate school, where she gained the expertise that had brought her to a conference on women and human rights. Our backgrounds were totally different, right up to the year or two before we met, but from those backgrounds we had followed two routes to the same dream of a changed future for women. Surely we have all had such experiences of oneness with all kinds of people — young, old, male, female, white, black, educated, illiterate, and so on — in life and work. Such encounters not only convinced me of the strength of our growing network of women dedicated to a better future for all but also gave me strength to invest even more energy into the enterprise.

⁂

The special perspectives brought by some of the younger members of our staff and network especially helped me in the area of communications technology. I learned so much from them. For instance, a very thoughtful and computer literate young woman, along with some of her friends, set up our first database system for grants management. As I was attempting to become computer literate myself, I would fuss and wonder about the magic of the new technology, and this young woman gave me some great advice: "Anne," she said. "Instead of trying to understand how the computer works, just use it! You talk on the telephone all the time. Do you understand how the telephone system works?" Her words helped me greatly then, and they still guide me as I relate to new technologies.

With that database in place, we were able to keep track of every request and inquiry that we received from women's groups around the world. The requests were just trickling in at that time. But I wanted to have the best database system possible so we could use and learn from this information — basic information about hundreds and ultimately thousands of women's groups around the world. "Communications, media, and communications technology" was one of the areas of emphasis in our early grant-making program, so it also had to be part of our day-to-day operations. Expanding networks of women, enabling the broad sharing of ideas and experiences, and encouraging women's participation in the communication revolution were all part of our mission.

The experience with my computer mentor, as well as a subsequent experience with a young volunteer who asked to apprentice with me and who ultimately became our fund-raising manager, led me to hire many very young people, people embarking on their first real job. Their minds were open as they interacted with women around the world, and that openness and desire to learn became part of the style of The Global

Fund too. What these young people lacked was experience, which they could gain from their interactions with many women as they increasingly represented The Global Fund at meetings around the globe.

A couple of board members questioned my hiring so many young people and particularly my giving them real responsibilities; the board members accused me of doing this in order to maintain power. This suggestion surprised and saddened me, not only because they missed the point of my actions but because they demeaned the wonderful contributions of these young staff members. Simply put, my reasons for hiring such young people were that they had fresh perspectives, they were not likely to second-guess the women who were writing to us from around the world, and they brought different experiences and expertise that greatly benefited the organization. Perhaps most important, the young staff people were especially eager to learn from the women who wrote to us. I believe that this attitude added significantly to our effectiveness and to our message of respect and empowerment for women we worked with globally.

Often, when I was invited to speak about our grant-making program or about women's groups around the world, following our principles of diversity and competence, I would strongly suggest or even insist that the younger program officers do the speaking. They knew the programs best. When we were invited to international conferences, notably all of the regional conferences leading up to the Fourth World Conference on Women, held in 1995 in Beijing, China, younger staff members represented The Global Fund around the world. I attended an occasional meeting, but for the most part these younger staff members were out there being The Global Fund in public.

The difficult exceptions were when I was invited to speak at meetings that we believed might provide us with an important pool of donors, and our fund-raising manager would insist that I or a particular staff or board person do the speaking. We tried to keep in mind that we wanted to be effective in many ways, including fund-raising. Conflicting priorities, such as this one between our need to raise funds and our desire to empower other staff members and diversify our public presence, are unavoidable, but they can be acknowledged, considered, and addressed openly.

Developing an Organizational Style

The management style of The Global Fund became of paramount importance to me, and that style was very personal. What I mean by *style* probably harks back to the days when I worked at Stanford University Press, where *The Elements of Style* by Strunk and White advised simplicity, clarity, and modesty.[2] Another writer, Sir Arthur Quiller-Couch, defined literary style in this way: "This, then, is Style...essentially it resembles good manners. It comes of endeavouring to understand others, of thinking [of] them rather than [of] yourself — of thinking, that is, with the heart as well as the head. It gives rather than receives; it is nobly careless of thanks or applause, not being fed by these but rather sustained and continually refreshed by an inward loyalty to the best."[3] Developing a style in your program or organization, then, has to do with leadership that is open to suggestion and correction, leadership that can learn, that can be modest, and that can emerge from different parts of an organization.

Having a set of guiding principles allows you to attain this kind of style and to be intentional about the work. I wanted our belief in the empowerment of the women who were our grantees to hold true for those who worked for The Global Fund directly, as well as for our donors and volunteers. I applied this belief to the processes and structures of the organization, developing a management style that was dedicated to empowerment in all parts of the organization.

Although I had managed teams and various programs before beginning The Global Fund, I had never previously started an organization. Feeling inexperienced in management, I thought I should read up on the subject. This I did by borrowing numerous books and reading about theories of management. I learned that the style of The Global Fund already expressed much of what was in the current literature on organizational theory; it embodied the idea of a "learning" organization, of various loci of responsibility, of respecting each employee for what she had to offer, of an organization operating in terms of guiding principles, and of using new and "softer" ways of managing.

Three years into the life of The Global Fund, one of our donors who was also a management consultant brought to my attention the work of Peter Senge[4] and asked me whether I had based The Fund on some of his ideas. I had not read Senge's work, but when I did I realized that The Global Fund already exemplified some of his key ideas for more effective organizational growth, such as: approaching one's life and work as a creative activity, holding a personal vision, committing to the truth, recognizing our connectedness in the world, compassion, and constant curiosity and learning.

In my reading, however, I found very little on the actual application of these ideas in a real organization, and this is one of the reasons that I decided to share my experiences in this book.

I found few published works that gave me insight into the nuts and bolts of putting principles into practice. Furthermore, as far as I could tell, many of the people writing books on nonprofits in particular had never founded a nonprofit organization or run one for any period of time.

The models of organization that I read about as I was developing The Fund stressed action and learning over rigid planning; in this regard, again, I found that The Fund was on the cutting edge of organizational development theory. We were clear about where we were headed but flexible about how to get there. This meant that we were able to take advantage of opportunities, responding to the individual interests, skills, and leadership of staff members, volunteers, and other people who crossed our path.

Some of the principles that came to characterize the organization were not as commonly discussed or agreed upon by management consultants, but they turned out to contribute to the success of The Fund. For example, as I have noted, we believed in being evenhanded and transparent throughout the organization. This included treating all donors equally, rather than according to a hierarchy of giving. Most fund-raising experts advised that in order to "push people up" to higher levels of giving, it was necessary to categorize them in terms of how much they had given. I did not want to do this because I thought that it would separate rather than bring together our donors and would go against our principle of treating everyone in an evenhanded way. Therefore, except for the first eighteen months when we had created a group of founding donors, we listed all donors in alphabetical order in our annual reports, with no reference to the amount of money they had given. We included a statement at the top of the list of donors that said the following:

Dear Friends: It is customary for not-for-profit organizations to list their donors by category (such as "patron," "benefactor," or "golden giver," noting in all cases what level of giving the donor "fits." At times we have been advised by fund-raisers that we ought to fit our donors into a hierarchy, but we think otherwise. We see the supporters of The Global Fund as part of a network of equal partners. We hope each and every donor is reaching to the limit of her/his capacity to join with us and with women overseas to make a difference.[5]

This approach brought mixed reactions. Some donors very much appreciated this evenhanded approach because they liked being seen as part of our community rather than separated off as "rich" supporters. Other people wanted special recognition for their gifts, and no doubt some of those people did not give to The Global Fund in those early days. Some wanted us to use their funds in ways that limited our freedom or did not focus directly on the mission of the organization. Standing up to and prevailing in the face of such pressures was challenging. Sometimes having to turn down money because of a conflict with principles risked losing relationships or not meeting the budget. In the end, however, having a set of guiding principles was very helpful in clarifying our day-to-day work and being able to explain why we did what we did.

Remaining Open and Willing to Learn

As The Global Fund grew and developed, the "learning" style of the organization served us particularly well; "learning" became a central guiding principle.

In practical terms, here is how we operated: we listened

carefully to everyone — grantees, staff, donors, board, advisors — and we planned in terms of what we heard and learned. For example, we undertook to develop a series of "Women, Money, and Empowerment" workshops in response to requests from groups of women who believed they had something to learn from us about fund-raising. We initiated study circles on various topics, including trafficking in women and girls, in response to the heartfelt interests of some donors who wanted to learn and do more on the topic. Our grant-making was entirely responsive; we learned from women about their problems and we sought to respect their solutions. In the fund-raising program, we learned from volunteers and donors as we related with them. Our strategic planning welcomed change and modification. We had a small staff that worked well together; we got up in the morning eager to get to work and to work hard. The Fund had an atmosphere that was open, interesting, and fulfilling, in which we could all learn from each other and be in a place that was the way we wanted the world to be.

Although a number of metaphors have come to mind in describing The Global Fund at various points in its development, the one that worked best for me in the end was of the organization as a garden. The Fund was not a formal garden, but rather a wild green one that was healthy and vital, where lots of wonderful things were growing and where life was constantly beginning and ending. It was a place where diversity was necessary in order for the whole to be healthy, a place where seeds could be sown or could flutter in to find fertile ground. Some gardeners might move to the edge and cultivate new ground, some might water and fertilize the more established parts of the garden, and some might nurture more fragile plants. Growth, life, and energy were to be found in such a place. I also saw that, like any garden, The Global Fund was only a tiny part of a bigger world where everything is interrelated.

This metaphor allowed for change and creativity, and it also allowed for freedom. As I began to share it with others, I found that it appealed very much to women around the world, especially women who wanted to believe that life could be beautiful, that connecting, learning, and treating each other well, with respect and love, could be transformative.

Things to Remember
as You Cultivate Your Dreams

- Create a list of beliefs or principles that will guide your work.

- Give these ideals reality every day.

- Allow processes and structures to develop that are consonant with these ideals.

- Know where you are going but remain flexible about how to get there.

- Learn from everyone and everywhere, from experience and feedback.

CHAPTER SIX

Grow Strong and Stay Lean

—— ❦ ——

Organizations, like people, die from overeating rather than from staying lean.

— Bill Hewlett

By the time we reached our fifth year, The Global Fund had grown from a tiny group of women intent on creating a new funding organization into an extensive network spanning the world and involving relationships with hundreds and even thousands of individuals and groups. We were seeing the value of interconnectedness through our web of donors, grantees, advisors, board members, businesspeople, foundation officers, friends, and volunteers. Women's groups were brought to our attention by advisors; grantees became advisors and board members;

donors became volunteers and advisors; grantees became donors. We all became both givers and receivers.

Our way of doing business — applying our values and principles to the day-to-day life of our organization — was proving to be effective. We were getting the job done very well, being accountable, and at the same time being good to one another and treating each other with respect, evenhandedness, and trust.

We found that as we sought to strengthen and empower women everywhere, we needed strength and empowerment too, and we received plenty of that from the grantees and volunteers who reminded us that we were not isolated as we worked to better society. We also received inspiration from our donors, especially those who shared our vision at the very beginning, offering flexible funds for the first steps toward our plans and vision. We greatly valued these relationships. These donors trusted us, just as we trusted our grantees, and this was a lovely way to work. Because we were donors ourselves, we knew how difficult it could be to choose to fund one organization rather than another and how distasteful it is to be treated purely as a source of money and not as a valued partner working toward a shared vision.

My original concept for The Global Fund was that it would be a kind of guerilla operation, staying very small and nimble, perhaps encouraging or even spinning off other women's funding agencies around the world, rather than just growing bigger and bigger itself. In the beginning, in 1987, I even had the idea that The Fund would be a project; we would give away about ten million dollars by the year 2000 and then go out of business, having strengthened many women's groups.

Given this original idea of the organization, I tried over the years to resist building a bigger and more permanent and predictable structure for The Global Fund. But the dynamic growth of The Fund could not be denied. More and more women's groups wrote to us, and more and more donors generously provided support. Every few months it became clear that the staff was overworked and that we needed more help. And every time we added a new staff person, the work increased.

As your program or organization expands and grows, how do you manage that growth? Should it be encouraged? Is growth always desirable? Growth can be a sign of health, but it can also present problems. As it happened, The Global Fund doubled in size in terms of budgets, groups assisted, and staff every year for the first five years. Once, while on a trip, I glanced at a complimentary copy of *Fortune* magazine in my hotel room and learned that the growth rate of The Global Fund was faster in those first few years than the growth rate of the fastest growing corporations in the United States. (Unlike the corporations the article profiled, however, we weren't working with budgets of multimillions at that point; we were just dealing with hundreds of thousands of dollars.) Instead of embracing growth for growth's sake, I tried to focus on creating and maintaining a balanced, open environment in which good things could happen, a place where we treated each other well, where we accomplished our work efficiently and effectively, and where our processes and structures reflected our principles.

I was greatly influenced by a conversation I had with Bill Hewlett, the cofounder of the Hewlett-Packard Company and someone I had known through my work at the Hewlett Foundation. During The Global Fund's first year, I met with Bill to ask him for advice as well as support. He gave me both. Among other questions, I asked him this: "Please give me whatever advice you have about creating a successful international organization." He replied with the quote that opens this chapter: "Organizations,

like people, die from overeating rather than from staying lean."
He also counseled me to focus as closely as possible on vision and
purpose and to perfect our programs before adding anything
more. He asked why we were not focusing on a particular region
of the world, why we were starting out with the whole world. I
said that I thought that improving the status of women couldn't
be done effectively with a few successes here and there; instead,
we needed to work for women everywhere, to strengthen the
worldwide women's movement. I went on to say that we were
trying to focus in other ways — on processes (seeding, strengthening, and linking groups, particularly those that were working
on difficult and controversial issues) and on style (doing our
work consciously, to build relationships).[1] He saw the point —
we weren't focusing geographically, except to focus on groups in
poorer countries, but we were definitely focusing. He again emphasized the extreme importance of doing what one plans to do
very well before adding any other activities.

While the growth of The Fund was surely a positive thing —
of course we wanted to help as many people as possible — we
knew that growth is not synonymous with success and that it can
pose significant challenges. Indeed, I had been struck by a line by
Edward Abbey, quoted in Richard Douthwaite's book *The Growth
Illusion*: "Growth for the sake of growth is the ideology of the
cancer cell."[2] I hope that some of the experiences described in
the paragraphs that follow will be helpful to you as your efforts
gain momentum and grow.

One step that I took in the third year of The Fund was to
apply the learning principle and turn to some experts to help me
think about how to manage what seemed to be inevitable and
rapid growth. Hearing an outside perspective on the work of an
organization is always helpful. A team of four Stanford Graduate

School of Business alumni made themselves available to me on a voluntary basis to study our situation and provide advice. After some time and several consultations, they helped me to realize that I had to find ways to replace two of our three staff members with people who were more experienced, particularly in accounting and finance. I also needed to begin to develop formal personnel procedures and manuals. I had not really accepted that our informal little group was beginning to be a real organization and needed different kinds of expertise and administrative practices. The business school alumni group helped me accept that change.

Managing Stress

When an idea, program, or movement rapidly takes off, it taxes existing structures and resources. Staff members, in particular, face a variety of stressors. Whereas they used to work in relative obscurity, as their organization grows they may now feel that many eyes are on them. Increased requests for help and greater exposure to need can drain them emotionally. Amounts of space, materials, and personnel that seemed adequate last month can suddenly cease to be so, creating daily wear and tear.

Certainly, rapid growth during The Global Fund's early years caused stress among the staff. We were constantly working too hard and, though we loved what we were doing, it still felt like too much at times. I knew that a part of good management involved managing stress, but how was it possible to recognize the need soon enough and take the time to deal with it? Even though the staff met weekly and sometimes shared meals together, we also put in place a number of coping strategies. These included taking time off or meeting spontaneously for a nice cup of tea (stopping for tea was a kind of time-out my mother had instilled in me). Nevertheless, there were times when one could feel the strain: individual staff members behaved in uncharacteristically discourteous ways to one another; sometimes personnel procedures that we usually followed fell by the wayside; and occasionally a staff person would insist that doing something was not her job. I thought about all of this and concluded that under stress, some of us were becoming less rather than more flexible, and this rigidity was not at all the style that we wanted at The Global Fund. I found this mildly annoying. After all, we were not refugee women facing a daily struggle for life; we were a staff of people living in California and doing work that we loved. I was not particularly sympathetic to what I might have described as whining.

A wise and critical word from a staff member woke me up. I began to realize that stress had been mounting because many things were changing. The Fund was now almost eight years old, we had moved to a new office, we were receiving more and more grant proposals, greater numbers of donors were interacting with us, two staff members were soon leaving to move on to other challenges, and so on. I thought about all of this and about how I lacked a good understanding of what was going on with the staff. The helpful staff member pointed out to me that although the staff members all loved their jobs, they were in fact employees. They were dedicated, but they were not necessarily driven, as I continued to be.

After thinking about all of this for a while, I asked everyone to indulge me for a few minutes during one of our regular staff meetings, as I tried to put into words what was on my mind about stress: "We are not going through rape and destruction. We are not refugee women with our children, trying to find a new home. We are not living in Bosnia or Rwanda, trying to survive intact. But," I continued, "I finally recognize that we are going through significant changes, and you'll be glad to know that I realize this and we need to acknowledge it and do something about it."

After saying this, I went around the circle of staff and reviewed all of the particular changes that members were coping with. One was concluding her time as a full-time staff member, planning to become a consultant in two or three months; one was taking on additional responsibilities, especially with regard to the physical move to a new office; one was on a long tour of jury duty, coming into the office over the weekends to stay on top of her work; one was coping with a difficult personal situation at home; and so on.

"In times of stress," I continued, hoping I was on the right track, "we should go back to the first principles of The Global Fund and be 'feminist,' in the sense of being open to gentle ways of working and interacting with each other. We should not allow ourselves to be unbending and rigid, which is so much more tiring than being flexible and softer." I went on to suggest that we should be much more conscious of and open to each other, expressing our feelings, reaching out to each other, and especially following the procedures that made life easier for everyone. We needed to consciously be more courteous and caring in the face of stressful situations. We talked about all of this and agreed that we would consciously think of each other rather than ourselves, that we would consciously be less rigid. Writing about this, I am reminded of this quotation attributed to Lao Tzu: "People at birth are soft and supple; at death, they are hard and stiff. When plants are alive, they are green and bending; when they are dead, they are dry and brittle....Soft and bending is the way of the living;

hard and brittle is the way of the dying.... So the arrogant and unyielding will fall; and the humble and the yielding will overcome."[3] In times of stress, return to softness; avoid rigidity.

Over the years, as the staff grew in size, we tried to embody Lao Tzu's wisdom by maintaining little rituals to keep the office soft and friendly. We honored birthdays with a cake or a sweet tart and requested that the birthday person share newfound wisdom. We took time out to honor staff members or volunteers after they had finished a particularly challenging project or job. Every now and then we spontaneously closed the office early and took an afternoon off. All participated in such happenings evenhandedly, and staff members introduced their own ideas for ways to deal with the increasing workload that came with the growth of The Fund. Our weekly staff meetings were structured to provide time to share our future plans, important work, and related necessary tasks, and also to allow time to remember that we were human beings working together toward a common vision — we were people who had personal lives that brought both joy and problems. Our decision to share our lives more readily provided these meetings with a much greater purpose than checking in on work; they allowed us to practice our principles of respect and caring for others.

Maintaining Vision

Perhaps even more important than the stress that rapid growth imposes on staff is the possibility that such growth can jeopardize a group's initial vision. A mission can become diluted or compromised. For example, once an organization becomes known for doing good work, donors may begin to try to "dump" money into what seems to be a thriving enterprise, and too much money can begin to blur the vision. If you are in the fund-raising business, you might say, "Give me a break, Anne. Too much money? That's the kind of problem I would love to face." Perhaps. Suffice it to say that I have observed several instances of organizations not being able to resist taking money for programs, spreading themselves thin, and losing sight of their precious vision. The chance to do something unanticipated can take one's eye off the original intent, and one can become less effective by trying to do too much for too many too quickly.

I remember that in the third year of The Global Fund, we were asked to cosponsor an international conference on women and serve as the fiscal agent for the million dollars that the organizers planned to raise. That amount was more than our budget at the time, and it was tempting to take on a very visible project that would also bring additional funds. But then Bill Hewlett's comment came to mind. I knew that such a project would be "the tail wagging the dog" and would distract us from our primary purpose. We were not in the business of running conferences. Our business was to raise money and give it away to women's groups around the world for work that they defined. That is what we needed to do — and do very well. Needless to say, we did not take on the project.

❧

When growth is very rapid, it is tempting to continually measure change in terms of the amount of money coming in or going out, rather than focusing on the positive changes that are taking place, the amount of progress being made toward your vision. I tried consciously to respond to people who asked, "How is The Global Fund doing?" by indicating that many more groups of women were forming, that networks around the world were expanding, and so on, rather than answering in the way that seems to be the norm, that is, by discussing how much our budget had grown. After I had retired from The Global Fund, when I asked that question of one of The Fund's board members, I received the immediate reply, "We raised xx million dollars last year." That wasn't really the answer to my question, or at least I didn't think so. Of course, I know most people want a short answer to such questions, and many of them want an answer that gives some measurement of how the organization is doing. So how *can* change be measured? In the next chapter we take up the issue of evaluation.

Over the years I have been very concerned about the extent to which nonprofit organizations have been driven by money. They often do more than measure themselves by how much money they raise — they define themselves by it. I have seen organizations that have had great success in fund-raising become more narrow and turn inward, as board members and even staff begin to think that their fund-raising success also means that they are somehow wiser than others and that they know more about the programs on the ground than the very people who are out there, at the grass roots. A major concern of mine is that more often than not money drives the agendas of nonprofits. As a result, the innovation and independent creativity of such organizations are lost to society. Money is useful, of course, but it is not the basic stuff of social change. It is compost for the garden, not water. Commitment and clarity of vision are the essential life-giving ingredients that will result in success, however you may define that term.

Nevertheless, when an organization is growing, most people believe that having more and more money is a sign of health and success. Sometimes it is, but often the opposite is the case. I re-call John Gardner's comment when he gave his farewell speech as the first chairperson of the Independent Sector, in 1983: "You have often heard me say that institutions are created by individuals to serve some clear and lively purpose, some compelling vision, and that they usually end up serving the purposes of institutional self-enhancement. We don't just want to grow big and strong. We want to serve the vision that stirred us in the first place."[4]

We at The Fund knew we could not do everything for everyone, and that if we tried to do so, we would run the risk of diluting our program. As your efforts gain momentum and you begin to raise money, more and more donors will be interested and want to support you. If your experience is anything like mine, people will see that you are an effective leader, and they will want you to take on projects that may be related to but not directly supportive of your vision and mission. They may even offer to provide funds for such efforts. Sometimes such suggestions can strengthen your program; more often than not, however, they will distract you from your clear vision and your chosen mission. Be careful about such opportunities.

As I mentioned in the previous chapter, I have found that turning down money can be very empowering; you recognize that the potential donor is generous, and you may suggest that they give their funds to another organization. The more you know about what you are doing and why and how you are doing it, the better your management and leadership will be. I am not talking about dogmatic adherence to your own ideas; I am talking about clarity of vision and purpose. A donor once approached me to ask if she could give The Global Fund a substantial grant to benefit Native American women within the

United States. At the time, we were not doing grant-making within the United States, but we knew of other organizations that were working with Native American people, and we directed the donor to those groups.

Developing and Maintaining Programs amid Growth

While striving to keep our eyes and ears open, to be a learning organization and remain flexible, we also had to focus our efforts with an effective framework. The Fund's grant-making program achieved such focus by continually assessing the changing needs of our constituents and refining the criteria we used to make decisions.

The grant-making process was an international collaborative effort shaped by our staff, our advisors and board members, and most important, by the grantees themselves. At the very beginning, we identified three areas of concern relating to women: human rights; communications, media, and modern communications technology; and economic autonomy. Grants ranged from five hundred to five thousand dollars, and were given to groups outside of the United States that were governed and managed primarily by women.

Here's how the process worked: When our office received a request for support from a group, our grants managers reviewed it, logged it into our computer system, and then made an initial decision about the appropriateness of the request to The Global Fund's program. If a group's work did not match The Fund's program, we notified their representatives promptly so that they could pursue other sources of funding. (For example, the group may not have been governed and managed primarily by women, or the group may have been working within the United States. Our criteria excluded such groups.) When possible, we tried to recommend other sources of funding more suitable for the request.

We then reviewed the remaining grant proposals again, and we requested additional information from the applicants. Before each board meeting, we drew up a descriptive list of all of the proposals under review, and we distributed this list to all members of our advisory council and board, whom we asked to comment on the requests. If a group's proposal was complete, endorsed by advisors, and appeared to match our program, the staff prepared background information for the board's discussion and recommended that The Global Fund provide a grant. This background information included descriptions of the group's goals, activities, structure, and request, as well as the larger policy issues that the proposal might raise. When the board approved a grant request, the staff promptly informed the group by sending out a grant letter, essentially a contract stating that the group would do what they said they would with the funds. (Each group was required to provide a report on the use of funds within about a year.) Soon after a grant was approved, other grantees, our advisors and donors, and other friends of The Fund were informed of the board's decision.

By The Fund's fifth year, requests for funding came to us at the rate of two or three a day, and Laurie Laird and Misti Mukhopadhyay, our grants managers, worked to capacity. They did their work so well that it looked easy, but they were managing huge amounts of information and producing the equivalent of three or four large books (of descriptions of groups) each year. To guide our selection decisions, over the years we had developed the following criteria:

- The group had to demonstrate a clear commitment to women's equality and female human rights as well as a concern about the way women are viewed and view themselves in society.

- The group had to be governed and directed primarily by women.

- The request had to be from a group of women working together rather than from an individual.

- The group had to have a strategy that would strengthen its work over time, and this was to be described in the proposal. (In other words, the proposal would offer answers to these questions: How will a grant from The Global Fund enable the group to reach its long-term goals? How will such a grant strengthen the group's programs?)

- A group that was known (by advisors and/or other credible contacts) to be effective on behalf of women was at an advantage. However, there were occasions when we made grants to entities that were not known to our advisors, and some of these grants turned out to be exemplary. (I am thinking here of a very early grant to a group of women working on HIV/AIDS in Africa; our small grant was all that they needed to move forward, form an organization, and be introduced to other funders. They soon became an important network of women working on AIDS across Africa.)

- A group that was just beginning or that may have needed initial financing was usually given preference over groups that had access to more established funding sources.

While it was important to us to remain open, flexible, and adaptable, these criteria allowed us to be very clear with women around the world about what we were trying to accomplish and what we needed to do in order to be accountable ourselves. The criteria fitted with our mission and intent in the sense that we wanted to learn from grant applicants about what they planned, how they defined issues, and so on. And, of course, the criteria allowed us to make decisions very quickly in the face of limited resources.

It was tempting to learn more from grantees and to provide the board and others with lots of information, but we resisted that temptation and tried to keep our process very simple. An experience that helped me value simplicity happened at my Tai Chi Chuan class one evening. As I was having some difficulty moving from one pose to the next, I asked my instructor, "How do you get from this pose to the next? What are the moves?" His response was immediate and straightforward: "Do nothing extra. Simply move from here to there, only using what you need. Nothing extra." After that, "nothing extra" became a kind of principle for us at The Global Fund. When we asked potential grantees for more information, we would ask only for the information that we truly needed to make a thoughtful decision. In many aspects of The Fund's work, "nothing extra" became a watchword; from the beginning we had eschewed complicated bureaucracy. "Nothing extra" fitted our style.

By providing potential grantees with an outline for a proposal and a list of the criteria for selection, we hoped that we were also offering them a model proposal for their interactions with other organizations and funders. (Since we published this information in our annual reports, we hoped that the model would help other people too.) A group's responses to the questions outlined in our criteria added up to a simple business plan or proposal. In the very early years of The Fund, when we outlined a typical proposal and a set of evaluation criteria, our intention was to provide this kind of assistance to groups that may never have written to an organization outside of their own country before. The template that we provided to potential grantees followed almost exactly the layout that we used when we wrote proposals to our foundation supporters.

In our decision making we depended to a great extent on the members of our advisory council who were located around the world. If opinions about a group differed, we would look first to the advisors who were located in the same country or region as the group. Over time, many people from grantee groups became advisors, and women began to work together to obtain support for women's groups in their countries and regions.

Our goal, our challenge, was twofold: we wanted to be able to raise enough money to respond to all of the worthy requests we received, and we also wanted to encourage other donors to begin funding women's groups at the grass roots. We did not seek to be big enough or rich enough to be the only resource in town; we wanted instead to foster such capabilities far and wide. We therefore shared our processes, our templates, and our database formats with other donors at meetings and workshops, and we encouraged other foundation officers and donors to get into the field and see for themselves that smaller women's groups can and should receive funds, that they were reliable and effective agents of change.

By June 1991, the end of our fourth year, we reached a major milestone: The Global Fund had given away more than one million dollars to women's groups internationally! Even though we tried to avoid measuring change in dollars, moving from nothing to a million dollars seemed significant. Equally exciting was the regional diversification that had occurred during this period. Fiscal year 1991 saw our first grants to eastern Europe, as well as much greater activity in Africa, Asia, and the Caribbean. We had supported more than 150 groups by this time. To give you a sense of their variety, and of our criteria in action, here are some examples of the many different groups we assisted:

- The Circulo de Feministas Cristianas (Circle of Christian Feminists) was established to question the persistence of sexism within religious institutions. This group of church women in Peru supported efforts to eliminate violence and discrimination against women. They conducted workshops, created exhibitions, and scheduled periodic days for reflection on such issues as women and violence, women and poverty, pornography, and reproduction. The group believed that a feminist analysis of religion was essential to the liberation of Peruvian women. Several advisors to The Global Fund who knew the work of the group strongly endorsed it, describing it as "excellent." The Global Fund approved a grant of five thousand dollars.

- The Katakala Women's Social Section Development Group was founded in 1988 by a group of women in six neighborhoods in Kampala, Uganda. The women wanted to create better conditions for women and children, and they began by focusing on women's health care. Over time, Katakala made the legal rights of women a greater concern. The group began a legal

aid service designed to educate rural women about
their legal entitlements, defend their rights, and form
paralegal women's groups in rural areas. Katakala
published leaflets and teaching manuals, managed a
mobile legal aid clinic, and carried out seminars in
leadership and management training for women.
Some seven hundred women participated in Katakala
activities. Global Fund advisors, two of whom were
directly familiar with the Katakala program, favored
support, and so The Fund provided a grant of $4,080.

- The Polish Feminist Association was started by women
from Warsaw University who were concerned that
women's rights were not being included in the policy
agenda of the nation at a time of intense social change.
Working entirely as volunteers, without outside financial
support, the group had begun to give a voice to women
on a variety of issues. The Global Fund for Women
approved a ten thousand dollar grant to the association.
Board members and advisors described the group as
"top notch but fragile and emerging and in great need
of support."

- The Kalyanamitra Foundation was created in 1985 by a
labor activist, two journalists, a lecturer, and two
psychologists in Indonesia who had each identified a
need for a women's voice in their fields of interest.
These women decided to create an organization to
strengthen other groups through documentation and
publications, networking, training, and research. Each
year, the group concentrated on a particular issue
relating to the rights of women, such as reproductive

health, violence, or legal rights. One year the focus was on rape. Through a national campaign, Kalyanamitra worked to reform Indonesia's criminal laws on rape, improve the implementation of such laws, and encourage the development of women's crisis centers throughout the country. It produced written materials, radio scripts, videos, et cetera to be disseminated through many other groups. Taking into account the positive responses from our advisors, we approved a ten thousand dollar grant.

As the requests increased, we were constantly trying to balance our fund-raising with the demand for help. At first, we focused more and more on women's groups that were clearly feminist in their approaches and that were working on more controversial topics. Over time, as we raised more and more money, we were able to increase the size of our grants from five thousand to ten thousand dollars and to support other groups that were a little more mainstream. My goal was to be there for any viable women's group that could not find support elsewhere; I wanted to strengthen the whole women's movement, worldwide.

❦

Although the grant-making program was central to our existence, we also developed two other programs — philanthropic education and fund-raising. I continued to conceive of The Global Fund as a catalyst, as a small, entrepreneurial organization that would stimulate other donors to get into the game of supporting women's groups. Thus, both the philanthropic education and the fund-raising programs were designed to increase money in the field in general. We sought to increase understanding among donors about women's concerns worldwide, and we also sought to support groups overseas that planned to create grant-making organizations designed to ensure the human rights of women.

The fund-raising program was designed to provide support for the work of The Global Fund and to identify, motivate, and advise donors. More specifically, this program had these two goals: secure enough money to support the grant-making, philanthropic education, fund-raising, and administrative efforts of The Global Fund itself; and attract a broad base of supporters, particularly those people who had never before given to women's activities overseas but who wanted to find a vehicle for their own philanthropy and an expression for their concern about global issues.

Reviewing the Work

Over the years, the work of The Global Fund often threatened to become overwhelming. Everyone on the staff was overworked all the time. Yet the requests kept coming and, fortunately, so did the donations. In 1994, as we looked forward to the United Nations Fourth World Conference on Women, to be held in Beijing in 1995, we decided to step back, assess our programs, and gain a sense of the changing context for our work. Partly because of our work but also because of changing times, thousands of new organizations had been created to work on women's issues; the international women's movement was blossoming, and we needed to be sure that we were being as useful as possible. Our board and staff had grown over the years, and it seemed time to pause and be very clear about our focus. Many donors had joined in our vision, and increasing numbers of institutional donors (foundations, businesses, and multilateral agencies, for example) had provided support as well as input on the many activities that The Global Fund could take on for the women of the world.

Most important, perhaps, the world had changed over the previous few years, and, perhaps because of the prospect of another UN women's conference, issues that had been somewhat invisible before were beginning to emerge. For all of these reasons we believed that formally reviewing our work was important.

Every organization needs to stop and assess itself from time to time. At The Global Fund, we certainly took opportunities at staff and board meetings and at other gatherings to question the relevance of our work in terms of our mission. But stopping to formally gather information from diverse sources and then to assess the context and the relevance of your work is a healthy process. How often should an organization do this? There is no perfect time to do it, but my experience suggests that most organizations wait a little too long before looking honestly at their own structures and processes and trying to figure out their current health and relevance. The assessment and planning process can be expensive, but we were able to obtain expert help from within our broad network.

We looked to our network for advice. Many people in it were acknowledged experts in our field of work. Others were interested, thoughtful people who were working at the grassroots level around the world. We wanted a diversity of perspectives, so we asked lots of people these kinds of questions:

- What are the global issues that we should be thinking about?

- What are the major issues affecting women?

- What are the major needs?

- What are women thinking and/or concerned about?

- How is The Global Fund for Women doing?

- What should we be doing differently?

The responses poured in: "We are in a time of major global shifts." "Changes in systems offer opportunities for women to participate more fully." "Hierarchical systems are breaking down, but new models have not emerged." "Violence proliferates." "All issues are women's issues." "Women are poor, tired, left out, violated, silenced." "Any assistance is useful, and the flexible and respectful work of The Global Fund is particularly useful." We listened to and read the extensive feedback we received. We tried to analyze all of it, to find patterns.

Trying to find a basis on which to proceed, we could see that there were some overarching women's issues — namely violence, reproductive health, and economic autonomy/poverty — that affected all women in all countries. We also knew that the problems were connected to structural dysfunction; the very structures of society were distorting the lives of both men and women. We had started out with these ideas when we began the organization, and they were reinforced during this review process. New issues and ideas also emerged: the greater possibilities for women to participate in political change, the importance of policy work, the importance of international networks that had grown greatly since the late

1980s, the possibility of creative and effective use of technology and communications.

Every time we thought about one issue we realized that it was connected to another; poverty, hunger, violence, sex trafficking, child labor, health, education, money, power, governance, policy, participation, legal rights, literacy — these human rights issues snaked in and out of each other, over and under each other, interrelating and affecting each other. Issues cut across all classes and races, yet issues expressed themselves differently in different places.

Attempting to grasp all of this and put it into words, into a plan, I kept coming back to a couple of simple ideas that were also structural: we needed to consciously treat one another with more respect and compassion, and all people needed to be empowered to define their own needs and solutions. In practical terms, I believed this meant that we needed to continue to concentrate not only on the way in which we did our work, but also on the way in which any organization that we came in touch with did its work, and the way we individually interacted with each other.

Yes, we could get on with the work itself — raising and giving away money — but because the issues were so interconnected, it seemed to me that we had to emphasize even more the underlying processes of interaction that could transform social relations. We needed to support the efforts of organizations to create community and connection, to nurture leadership, and to encourage inclusion, participation, and diversity. More and more, I focused on trying to give reality to the guiding principles. I was reinforced in my view that what we do is important, but the way we do our work — the principles that guide the way — can be transformative.

Things to Remember
as You Cultivate Your Dreams

- Before adding new programs or activities, be sure you are effectively doing what you set out to do.

- Move from here to there simply, with "nothing extra."

- Focus and perfect your systems; do not be distracted from your purpose.

- Manage stress with awareness, fun, compassion, softness, and ritual. Avoid rigidity.

- Consciously assess your adherence to your mission and examine the nature of your growth.

- Periodically and formally evaluate the context of your work and its relevance.

- Measure success in many ways, not just in terms of money.

- Turn down money that is inappropriate to your goals or principles.

- Change consciously; prepare for it and slow it when need be.

- Remember that what you do is important, but the way you do it is more important.

CHAPTER SEVEN

Govern, Manage, and Evaluate for Empowerment

God, give us serenity to accept what cannot be changed, courage to change what should be changed, and wisdom to know the one from the other.

— Fourteenth-century soldier's prayer

I have seldom met a founding executive of a nonprofit organization who delighted in her or his board of directors — individual members of the board, maybe, but not the board as a whole. If you are beginning a program or an organization, I advise you to think carefully about how to create an environment in which the different parts of the organization can work together with respect and very open communication.

Interacting with the board, the governing body of an organization, is a challenging and time-consuming task in general, but this is especially true in the early years of an organization, when the founding executive wants freedom and unquestioning support. Figuring out the appropriate relationship between the day-to-day staff of an organization and the board of directors, the group of wise people that any executive hopes to have supporting her, is an ongoing challenge that requires patience and attention.

Creating the Governing Board You Need

If you are going to put together a nonprofit organization in the United States, you have to create a governing board — a group that is financially and legally responsible for the organization. And even if you are organizing your efforts as a project rather than as an actual organization, an informal board or advisory group is a good idea. Individual board members may bring you just what you need — support, commitment, wisdom, work, and wealth — but dealing with the board is a time consuming and sometimes difficult set of activities.

In many organizations in the very beginning, the board often consists of the founders or the friends of the founders. Later, additional board members often include people who bring special perspectives or expertise. As you put together a board or a group of advisors, in the beginning and perhaps throughout the life of an organization, first and foremost you need to bring together people who are committed to the vision and mission of the organization and who bring a diversity of perspectives. Look for people whom you would like to meet regularly and talk with, particularly people with a sense of humor. After that, you need three things: wisdom, work, and wealth. Hopefully you will find all three in each individual board member.

By *wisdom*, I mean knowledge of the programmatic interests

of the organization, knowledge of finance and budgeting, experience with or knowledge of organizational development or policy matters relating to the work of the organization, as well as common sense.

By *work*, I mean willingness to respond when something is needed. Will the board member review a proposal or a piece of writing? Can she connect us to a good lawyer, who might offer pro bono help? Would he be willing to pick someone up at the airport if necessary? Can he come into the office to stuff envelopes? Will she serve as chair, secretary, or treasurer of the board?

By *wealth*, I mean the capacity to give significant financial support to the organization or else the willingness and ability to open doors to sources of money. Every board member must be willing to write a personal check to the organization. I remember once hesitating and really not wanting to give a donation to an organization on whose board I was serving; I felt that the budget was so high that my donation wouldn't make a difference. But I also believed that this was a clear test of my commitment to the mission and goals of the organization. I explained this to the executive and left the board. As a board member, you should regularly check your level of commitment; donating and being willing to give significant time to an organization are good tests of commitment. One experienced director I knew told me that he would not join a board if he found himself unwilling to write a check and give at least a day a month to the work of the organization.

In 1990, when The Fund was in its third year of existence, we invited Esther Hewlett to be the seventh member of the board, and she asked me what the board was like. She knew a great deal about the organization already; she had been working as a volunteer almost from the beginning. I said, "It's a great group, and board meetings are fun. We get together three times a year, usually in somebody's home in California or on the East Coast, decide upon grants, and discuss policy issues. We like each other. The discussion is always lively."

When she asked me to describe the other board members, I felt proud of the talented group of women we had assembled: Dame Nita Barrow, a nurse by profession and the representative of Barbados to the United Nations and soon to become governor-general of that country, an international figure, large in body and heart, a wise woman; Kaval Gulhati, former president of the Center for Development and Population Activities, knowledgeable on international women's issues and organizational management, a consultant spending half of her time in India and half in Washington DC; Frances Kissling, head of Catholics for a Free Choice, smart, intellectually curious, committed to women's causes, contentious, and articulate; Laura Lederer, working at that time at the Skaggs Foundation, intense, committed to women's causes, particularly more difficult issues such as pornography, focused on writing on feminist issues; and Marysa Navarro-Aranguren, historian at Dartmouth College focused on the Latin American women's movement, born in Spain, a Basque, also a Latina, having spent years in Argentina and Uruguay, a passionately committed feminist. I was the sixth board member, a New Zealander who had lived most of my life in the United States and Canada, knowledgeable in the philanthropic and international development world, and president and cofounder (with Frances and Laura) of The Global Fund.

"Why me?" asked Esther. An active volunteer and a mother of three, at that time Esther did not see herself as a feminist. She had become the volunteer that I most often called upon for anything and everything a new organization needed, whether it was a place to house a visitor from overseas or a batch of cookies for a brown bag lunch. Esther and I had been luncheon companions for a long time, discussing international women's issues, even back in the days of my attempts to begin a women's program at the Hewlett Foundation. "We're building the board at the moment," I said. "I need help in the ongoing business of The Global Fund in California. I need a friend close at hand, and I need your quiet strength and support." Esther took all of that in and added with a smile, "And it wouldn't hurt to have the Hewlett name on the board, would it?"

Our beginning board members collectively brought to The Fund all of the attributes described above, which I consider much more important than having famous people on a board. Nevertheless, Esther was right: a well-known name helps an organization gain recognition. But it is no substitute for commitment, diversity, humor, and wisdom, work, and wealth.

Working through Differences with the Board

As it turned out, Esther's first board meeting was the first of several in which the fun went out the window and difficulties and painful interchanges came in. At least two of us ended up in tears, exhausted and frustrated. What had happened? Our little organization, innocent and beautiful, was beginning to grow up. The budget and program were expanding rapidly, and the staff and I were taking the lead, forging ahead, building an organization that was beginning to be known around the world, with a style of its own. Board members felt responsible, and at the same time they felt left behind. We had started out as a close little group, all working as volunteers. Now we had a small staff and a paid president and chief executive officer (me) who were actively creating the programs and the style of the organization. As staff leader, board member, and cofounder, I was at the center of all of this. Everyone began to feel stressed, and some reacted by becoming more rather than less rigid, making decisions and pronouncements in an attempt to feel in control.

Thinking of that time, I remember the nervousness I sometimes felt before each board meeting. I worried about what hoop some of the board members would put me and the rest of the staff through. I had my own ideas about what the organization should be, and I was working day and night to bring it all together. Board members met only three times (and later two times) a year. It was annoying to have to answer to them. Everything about The Global Fund had been fun and creative at the beginning, but dealing with the board began to be work. Before each meeting, we staff members tended to get anxious, and before long our family and friends began to recognize the syndrome. On one occasion, my friend Barry, having already questioned my wisdom in even having a board, offered this thought: "Anne, your problem is that The Global Fund is a work of art for you, something you have created and are in the process of creating. You know what you want it to look like, and you don't want anyone else to mess up the composition."

When you have a dream and begin to try to make it a reality, it may very well be like a work of art, like a painting. You know what you want to do, and you have a vision of what your painting will look like. Feedback from others is welcome and useful, until it starts to encroach upon your vision.

A major reason to have a board of directors or a council of advisors is to be able to learn from them, to open up to diverse perspectives. But what you want from your so-called advisors above all is support and freedom. Over time, the excitement of creating the organization or project sometimes seems to be dampened by the very people that you have asked to join you, as they begin to feel responsible for the organization and/or want to have greater involvement and even control.

The work of art metaphor was interesting, at least more so than the one everyone else applied to the new organization; they called it "Anne's baby." I didn't subscribe to the "my baby" metaphor at all. Part of my vision for The Global Fund was that it would expand, growing beyond me, the founders, and the staff to include thousands of people. Such a vision took some years to realize. Whatever the metaphor, though, bringing the organization to a point of strength was very much a creative act for me, and I sometimes reacted to what I considered interference in my vision by being prickly, impatient, and defensive.

Each board member brought with her an approach and often an agenda that somehow had to be integrated into the work of The Global Fund. Enjoyable, exciting, and exhilarating times happened, as we witnessed each board member's strong commitment to empowering women and doing it in a way that was respectful and responsive. But there were frustrating and painful times too. Our joint commitment to a vision of women's empowerment held firm, thank goodness, and it carried us to the other side. But differing styles, inevitable and desirable because of our commitment to diversity, sometimes felt impossible to accommodate.

As the budget grew, some board members took a much greater interest in what we were doing. At one meeting in 1991, one board member declared, "Well, now that this little organization has a million-dollar budget, I guess I'll have to begin to take it seriously." She was half joking, but only half. The members of our small, hardworking staff were always invited to attend board meetings as observers or resource people, and the staff met after this particular meeting to talk about it. Their reactions included the following: "Didn't those board members take the organization seriously when we were giving away smaller amounts of money?" "Do they really see the organization as different now from the way we were before?" and "What does it matter how much money we are giving away? The spirit is the same." It pained me to see youthful idealism dampened; I hated to see the young staff disillusioned by the cynicism of some of their older colleagues. Such a diminution of the vision and style did not sit well with me. Nevertheless, without question the positive work greatly outweighed such disappointments.

For about eighteen months we struggled with differences in style among some of the board members and between some board members and the staff. The board is ultimately the responsible body in an organization; it is responsible for the fiscal health of the organization and for hiring and firing the chief executive. But such a hierarchical way of thinking about relationships was surely not the way we wanted to do things at The Global Fund, was it? It didn't fit with my vision of the way The Global Fund should look. At the same time, a pure consensus model, favored by some feminist organizations, seemed inefficient and out of sync with the way The Global Fund had actually unfolded. We had developed a style and structure that located responsibility in various parts of the organization, so that leadership and power could emerge from many directions. I noticed that people who took on increasing responsibility ended up having more power in the organization.

The metaphor of The Global Fund as my work of art didn't apply anymore; as The Fund moved from its beginnings to a more mature organization in which many people took responsibility and assumed leadership roles, it could no longer be seen as a piece of art, a composition, in the mind of any one person.

⚜

I had articulated in one of our meetings on board development that what The Global Fund needed was a "council of wise women." By that, I meant a group of people who could be called upon for their thoughts and advice upon the workings of the organization, always with love, respect, and caring. Certainly such a council would have responsibilities, fiscal and legal, as well as administrative, in the sense of hiring and firing the staff director. But the concept of the council would be quite different from that of a board of directors, which is often seen as a group of bosses who fly in two or three times a year and feel compelled to command and control.

The collaboration, cooperation, and caring at The Global Fund, which characterized our interactions with grantees, donors, staff, and advisors, did not describe the board as long as some board members had a hierarchical mindset and the need to wield power rather than to share it. At one point in all of this, as I discussed a particularly inappropriate request that one board member had made of me and the organization, another member of the board said, "Why don't you just lie to her? That would end the discussion." Both the inappropriate request and the suggestion to lie were unacceptable. But the suggestion reminded me of discussions I had had years before with Ruth Chance, an expert in philanthropy in San Francisco. Ruth said she believed that all too often, weak or bitter relationships with a board of directors led executive directors to lie about what was actually happening in their organization. As a member of many boards over the years, I have twice had the experience of being part of a board that had to fire the executive for misrepresenting to the board the situation of the organization. To avoid such circumstances, the staff leader needs to create a shared community based on such principles as transparency, openness, and respect.

One key to good relationships between the board and staff of an organization is ensuring a trusting, open, and completely honest relationship between the two groups, facilitated, I think, by a very close relationship between the chair of the board and the staff leader. In 1993 luchie pavia ticzon, who had been a grantee, then a member of the advisory council, and then a board member, became board chair. She and I went about creating an effective relationship by consciously agreeing to let each other know immediately if we had a question about a decision or conversation or if we felt in any way uncomfortable about any interchange, however trivial or important. Of course, we communicated regularly, and we set aside time to discuss in a very conscious way anything and everything about The Global Fund and its work. This very open and honest arrangement worked very well for the years prior to my retiring from The Global Fund.

<hr/>

Would I advise someone starting an organization to create a board or an advisory group? Yes, of course, because you must have a board in order to incorporate and become a legal nonprofit organization, at least within the United States. Yes, because you probably have to in order to raise money, to show that you are not alone in what you are doing. And a resounding *yes* because not only will you want to show that you are not alone, but in fact you do not want to be alone. Our problem in the early years of The Global Fund — and the problem of many other executives and boards these days — was that we had conceived of the board in a traditional way, as being located at the "top" of the organization. This hierarchical model, left over from the past, turned out to be inefficient and divisive. Like other parts of The Global Fund, the board needed to be valued for its unique responsibilities and included equally in our work through open communication and courtesy. We should have treated the board or board members as we treated donors, grantees, volunteers, staff people, and advisors — as equal members of our enterprise, rather than as our superiors. Much earlier, I should have worked to create much greater community between the board and staff.

It took a while, but we dealt with these imbalances within the organization. We did several things. At one board meeting, for example, Dame Nita turned to the other board members and, recognizing that there seemed to be problems or miscommunications, asked them, "What do you want from Anne and the staff? What do you expect of her and them?" There were several answers, all of which guided my subsequent actions. One in particular was this: Board members wanted more of my attention. They wanted to know that I was taking their suggestions seriously. They wanted to know that they were valued and listened to by me and by the staff. The message came through loud and clear. I instituted a more formal and more frequent method of communication between the staff and the board. I took much more time to be in touch with board members directly, to honor them for their help and ideas, and I tried to do this in public whenever possible.

In addition, we expanded the board to include several more board members from outside the United States. In particular, we invited people who had experience in developing feminist communities. They brought a gentler, softer style to the board, which reduced the command/control and competitive mentality that had occasionally unbalanced our work. We took more time at board meetings to speak about our personal lives and interests, and we lengthened the duration of meetings in order to give people who had to travel long distances more time to rest. That year and a half of misunderstanding and imbalance between the board and the staff was tough to get through. But it was a learning experience, and the measures we took to resolve those difficulties made The Global Fund stronger in the long run.

Managing and Evaluating Staff

In the meantime, our staff was growing, and this, too, required careful management. In the beginning, as I have mentioned, I hired many young people as interns, volunteers, and staff. I liked their energy and curiosity, the diversity that they brought to the organization, their knowledge of modern communications technology, and their belief that anything was possible. Almost all of these young staff people were fabulous; they were smart, innovative, and hardworking. On the few occasions that a staff person wasn't working out, she would choose to move on; it was just not possible to be working at The Global Fund in those early days and not pull one's weight. There was too much to do. In one case, I had to fire a staff person. I learned through this experience that honesty, clear communication, and decisive action were important. I made the mistake of allowing this person to stay on for several weeks after we discussed the need for her to leave. I should have asked her to leave immediately; it would have been easier on her and on the rest of the staff to limit the duration of the pain of separation.

As the organization grew, we needed to develop personnel policies and systems of staff evaluation. I borrowed from organizations that I had known and admired, adapting their personnel policies and evaluation procedures. We were determined to offer generous severance policies, health benefits, and as soon as possible, retirement benefits. This was unusual for a nonprofit start-up, but we wanted The Global Fund to model the principles of generosity and caring, and we believed that our employees, all women at that time, deserved the best benefits we could afford. If you plan to realize your dream through the creation of an organization, I recommend this approach to you. Generosity pays off; it comes back in many ways, most notably in that it makes your staff members feel valued, which leads to greater productivity, commitment, and a warm environment.

Evaluating staff members formally was an opportunity to take stock and think about whether the organization was serving the individual staff person well and vice versa. Staff members who had worked in other organizations let me know that they appreciated the method of staff evaluation we put into place. Here is how it worked: A few days before the annual staff review, the manager (at the beginning, that was me) and the staff member each received a form from the business manager that laid out a series of questions, asking about the staff person's goals and performance. The staff member and the manager filled out these forms independently and then planned a meeting, during which we each scanned the other's form. Usually our evaluations were very similar; in those areas where I thought a person needed to improve, she usually thought the same thing. Most important, though, since we each filled out the same form, during the actual staff review we were able to concentrate on each other's goals and comments rather than on our own. We were starting from a place of community.

We approached staff evaluation as partners, jointly discussing whether the individual staff person was meeting her goals. These meetings were good occasions to talk about the hopes and dreams of the staff person and whether The Global Fund was the ideal place for her. The meetings often reminded me of this quote from Antoine de Saint-Exupéry: "Life has taught us that love does not consist in gazing at each other, but in looking outward together in the same direction."[1] When a staff member was having problems doing her job well, we discussed why this was happening, whether she loved her job, and whether her personal goals were in sync with those of the organization. It was a time to come together, to connect. The principle of connection and integration, which we hoped would characterize the organization, was a route to empowerment for staff members as well.

Evaluating Programs

Our approach to program evaluation mirrored our approach to staff evaluation. Our major program was giving grants. We needed to find out how effective our grant-making program was, not only to improve our practices but also to be able to report back and be accountable to our donors.

As usual, we tried to manage and administer the money that our donors had entrusted to us in ways that would express the principles and values of The Global Fund. Dealing with money is too often seen as dealing with power. We tried to balance that perception of money as power by stressing that the strength and power of the grantees (their commitment, their energy, and their work) was equally important if not much more important than the money itself. Managing programs for empowerment involves truly learning and taking pleasure from the accomplishments of others — the staff, the consultants, the board, the advisors, and the people running the programs that your project or organization is supporting. Nevertheless, it is necessary to formally learn from your program and maintain a sense of accountability in program matters, especially if your program or organization is receiving money from various sources, including foundations and individuals.

At The Global Fund for Women, I had conceived of our grant-making program in various ways, sometimes seeing the grant maker–grantee relationship (or the relationship of the activist and the community that she serves) as a business arrangement between a company and a consultant or between a service provider and a client. At other times, in other moods, I have thought that the grant maker–grantee relationship is like, or perhaps is, a love affair. By this I mean that the grantee courts the grant maker through a process that is fun and exciting. And we all know that once the romantic pair gets married or makes some significant commitment, the best relationship is one in which each person respects the freedom and independence of the other, in which there is trust and a loving attempt at equality, in which each provides general support rather than project-specific support to the other. If you love someone, you give her or him what she or he requests, rather than what you determine she or he needs.

So one of the ways in which we promoted empowerment of individual women and women's groups overseas — the ultimate goals of our programs — was by providing flexible general support funds with as little bureaucratic interference as possible. Given the need for accountability, of course we required a letter of understanding and a report on the use of the funds. For new groups and groups in chaotic and changing societies, this approach was especially important. The less direction a funder imposes, the freer and more empowered the grantee is and the more effective that grantee can be.

I speak from the point of view of having run an organization that was both a grant maker and a grant seeker. The Global Fund as a grant maker gave small grants, up to ten thousand dollars, and tried to give them very flexibly, in terms of the stated needs of the grantee. We wanted to do unto others as we would have others do unto us. What did we want to have done unto us when we were acting as a grant seeker? We wanted the most flexible support possible, support that respected and empowered our judgments — in other words, general support.

Some people say that general support grants are impossible to evaluate. I would argue that any grant is hard to evaluate. It is just as hard to know what a grantee accomplished, truly accomplished, as a result of a specific project as it is to learn how a general support grant strengthened an organization. It may be easier for a grantee to report on a specific project than it is for an organization to report on the results of a general support grant over time, but it is an excellent management exercise for an executive to do so. Reporting on the difference that a general support grant has made requires a person to think of the progress of the organization as a whole, to think in integrated rather than fragmented terms.

The challenge of evaluating programs reminds me of the women I visited in Nepal with Rita Thapa, a Nepali women who later became a board member of The Fund. Women from various villages had assembled on a small hill, under a couple of huge trees. There must have been fifty or sixty women, almost all of them holding babies or children on their laps or hips, wearing thin cotton saris — red, blue, green, yellow, multicolored — and greeting us with smiles. Some of them had walked three or four hours to greet us, as they do every month or so to attend the meetings of their group.

Their group had formed as a by-product of a foreign donor–sponsored government program intended to urge individual women to start small businesses in their homes. A Nepali woman, who worked in other villages with other women, encouraged these women to come together occasionally to speak with each other and learn from each other. Each woman donated a few rupees to incorporate the group. They showed me with pride the sign and the small concrete building that they had built as their place to meet.

I asked Rita to pose a question to the gathered women. I wanted to know what they thought was the most important issue or problem for women there. They said that the greatest problem was that their husbands did not truly understand that they, the women, had aspirations for change; they wanted to learn, to grow, to become more. It was only with each other that they could discuss their hopes and dreams and plan programs and projects. I asked what their husbands thought, now that the women had formed their organization, built their building, begun to meet regularly to discuss problems, and begun to learn to read and write. They said that their husbands were proud of them. They liked to see that the women were happy. They felt good that the women had done these things.

The women's answers to my questions surprised me because most women I had met with in other parts of the world had answered the same question simply with "the need for money" or "violence." Instead, these women cut to the heart of all of the discussion that we had been having over the previous couple of years in the process of strategic planning at The Global Fund. They wanted to be understood and respected, and they wanted to determine for themselves how to make that happen. When these women gathered together, they shared stories and made connections that empowered them as much as or perhaps more than the specific program that had drawn them together in the first place.

As we drove home, Rita and I talked about our visit, and she told me that the government program on the formation of businesses had been terminated. The donor had conducted an outside evaluation, and the evaluators had concluded that the program had not resulted in sufficient measurable outcomes to warrant continuing it. It was, after all, a microloan program at its core — for that is what the experts had been saying the women needed — and the microloans had not resulted in sufficient economic outcomes to be judged successful in the time specified. Was this program a success or a failure? In strictly measurable terms, it was judged by the donor to be a failure, but in the minds of the women, who had created a strong community that empowered individual members, it was a success.

I have had seemingly endless conversations with foundation and government funders in the United States about how to measure the effectiveness of programs. I have undertaken plenty of evaluations myself and have found myself disillusioned most of the time. But some sort of evaluation is key to managing programs for change. My experience always brings me back to the importance of listening carefully to and learning from the people on the ground.

Evaluation is an ongoing topic among those who run non-profits. For the most part, individual donors will continue to support an organization if you can describe what has happened and tell stories about the effects of the program. But foundation officers want and need measurable evidence of the impact of the work. Most foundations, therefore, will insist on some sort of evaluation component in any program they fund. Most often, they need evaluation reports that both describe and measure outcomes. Most institutional donors, which are based for the most part in the United States, think in terms of results (the bottom line) rather than process.

I understand this approach very well. Having worked quite hard to raise money and set in place a program, I, too, wanted to have a sense of whether our work was worthwhile, whether it added up to something important. We had an idea that providing small grants to women's groups to do what they wanted to do, in the broad context of empowerment and women's rights, would be useful. Further, we had a hunch that women would feel more empowered just by creating groups and meeting together, sharing their ideas and experiences and connecting with each other. But how was it possible to demonstrate, let alone prove, this?

At The Global Fund I defined *empowerment* as "having a vision, having a plan to work toward that vision, and having the capacity to take the first steps toward the plan." The Global Fund's role in such empowerment usually involved responding to requests from women's groups to provide the financial means for women to take the first steps in a plan that they had already developed in the context of their vision.

In almost all cases, people who have a vision and a plan will somehow implement their heartfelt beliefs with or without money. We found over the years that the connection we made by linking with a group through the grant-making process was the more powerful force for change. By linking with women's groups through small grants, The Global Fund was saying, "You can do it. We, a worldwide network of caring people, believe in you and your heartfelt vision. We are with you." The ultimate benefits that come from people who are imbued with such a feeling are difficult to measure but possible to describe in stories.

In order to evaluate a program, you need to seek out key informants, and those key informants are the very people who run and benefit from the program at the most local level. Many foundations hire outside evaluators to gather information from these key informants, but The Global Fund opted to cut out that middle person and go straight to the source.

Therefore, our evaluation program, begun during the first year of The Global Fund, involved asking our grantees very directly how they thought their work had changed the lives of women in their group and in their community. If they could be specific about the difference our small grant had made, that was great. Frankly, if a group working on very difficult issues such as domestic abuse, rape, and genital mutilation had been able to continue operating over the course of the grant year, we considered that quite a success. From the beginning, we set in place a program that depended on self-reporting by grantee groups. To add credibility to our evaluation efforts and to draw on nearby expertise, I asked four knowledgeable people, all experienced evaluators, to serve as a volunteer evaluation committee to help us work out how we could learn from our programs and the grantees. The system depended on developing an environment of trust between the administration of The Global Fund and each grantee group.

We learned a great deal over the years. The evaluation program of The Global Fund did these four things:

- It provided feedback for the purpose of improving the management and administrative practices of The Global Fund itself.

- It gave grantees an opportunity to reflect on how The Fund's small grants made a significant and sometimes a measurable difference to the group and its future.

- It provided information about concerns and issues relating to The Fund's interests.

- It provided assurance to donors that resources were being used thoughtfully, efficiently, and with sensitivity.

The Global Fund asked each grantee to send us a final report, usually due a year after the grant was made. In the very early years, after reviewing the first thirty-five reports we received from grantees, our evaluation committee recognized that the questions we had posed as a framework for the required reports had grown out of our planning-implementation-evaluation model of development and did not always fit the processes employed by women running modest and effective grassroots organizations. Many of the overseas grantees stressed the coherence of the group itself — their commitment, their inclusiveness, and their vision — rather than specific goals. The specificity of our questions made grantees feel uncomfortable reflecting on qualitative changes, and we found that we were receiving reports that were not useful to us or to the grantees. Therefore we asked some of our grantees how we could modify our reporting questions, and we followed many of their recommendations, continuing to ask about goals and plans but adding questions about general outcomes, processes, and benefits to women. The reports from grantees then began to be much more useful and interesting.

For a while, in order to discern the long-term effect of support from The Global Fund, we tried out the idea of asking particular past grantees to report back about their ongoing work and progress. (We reimbursed them for providing us with this feedback.) We also experimented with a modest training program for advisors, board members, and staff to develop a protocol of policies and procedures for evaluation to use with some selected grantee organizations.

Later, in the early 1990s, we obtained a grant that allowed the Pacific Institute for Women's Health, based in Los Angeles, to visit some fifty-six grantees in eight countries and report on their successes, particularly with regard to health issues. Among many interesting insights — including the reality that in many languages there is no word for *empowerment* — the researchers learned that trust was a key element in women's perception of the success of their organizations. So important to these women were processes based particularly on the principle of trust that the researchers titled their report on the research project "Trust: An Approach to Women's Empowerment."[2] The researchers also discovered that the act of gathering together in groups with other women appeared to increase feelings of power, status, and well-being in women.

The Global Fund's advisory council, a group of about one hundred people who were active in the international women's movement, played key roles in evaluating groups and programs. Advisory council members helped us to determine whether or not to fund a particular organization, and then they helped us assess the success of grants and determine whether to continue our support. We started out inviting our friends and colleagues around the world to serve as advisors, and then we invited people from other international women's organizations to help us do informal evaluations. In time, the majority of our advisors came from the grantee groups themselves. In any assessment of a group, we would always depend first and foremost on advisors and grantees who were located in the region or country of the group — rather than on experts from far away — believing that people closest to the problems being addressed know best how to proceed. Our advisors, who were all volunteers, were key to our ability to operate around the world. Like members of the other groups that made up The Global Fund for Women, they served in many capacities: some were grantees, some were donors, and so on. We sought in many ways to blur the differences among us.

I must admit that it is difficult or even impossible to precisely measure the impact of what actually happened with the grantees of The Global Fund and with the organization itself. Were we to measure the impact of a grant on the women in that particular group or on their societies? Were we to measure the impact on donors and others who came in touch with activist women around the world? We could measure the increasing numbers of women's organizations that were forming, were growing, and were becoming increasingly active in country after country around the world, but what exactly would those numbers tell us?

Most of what we learned over the years was somewhat anecdotal. Our evaluation reports more often than not were a series of stories. The Zimbabwe Women's Resource Centre and Network grew in a few short years to become the focal center for work in that country relating to the 1995 Beijing women's meeting. With the help of The Fund, groups that began with three women became the first antiviolence centers in Belize and in Korea.

Women's funds were being formed and growing in every region of the world. As they multiplied over the years, these anecdotes and stories added up to powerful information and data that seemed to say that good things were happening as a result of our programs. The flexible and trusting style of The Global Fund was acknowledged as being unusual and effective by women's groups around the world.

❦

In the course of pondering this issue of evaluation and impact, I was lucky to come in touch with a renowned evaluator, Michael Scriven,[3] who had a deceptively simple formula for considering impact and effectiveness. He called it the *footprint approach*. As one walks across the sands of time and tries to make change (in our case, by making grants) one can leave different kinds of prints: the short but very deep footprint, which represents a deep impact on very few people; the long, thin footprint, which means a long-term impact on very few people; the wide but shallow imprint, which means a relatively superficial impact on many people; and so on. Presumably one wants to leave a big, fat, deep, long footprint, which would represent a deep, long-lasting, broad impact on a lot of people. But it is impractical to think that one can always do this. We need to understand our intentions as we implement programs and to be happy with whatever amount of impact we make, it seems to me.

Each of us needs to define what *success* means to us. Women everywhere are trying to make changes at different levels. A policy intervention may someday make a deep and significant impact on many people. Alternately, in the short term, paying for school fees for a single African girl could make a very deep impact on that one person and on her community and perhaps even on the wider world. We can succeed on many levels. If we see our programs as a business deal (between company and consultant or service agency and client), then we're probably hoping for a measurable outcome. If we see our program as a love relationship between an activist and the community he or she is serving, then we have other goals; we are intent on creating trusting relationships, and we seek to know that the members of the community are safe and happy, able to succeed in their own terms and to live and grow in freedom.

Things to Remember
as You Cultivate Your Dreams

- When putting together a board or advisory council, look for commitment, diversity, and people who provide wisdom, work, wealth, and a sense of humor.

- Work diligently to create a community among board and staff members.

- Form an open, trusting partnership between the board or advisory group leader and the staff leader.

- Let board and staff members know that they are valued; praise them in public and voice criticisms in private.

- Work from a place of community with staff members to learn whether their goals are being served as they meet the goals of the organization or program.

- Listen carefully to and learn from the people on the ground, those who are directly affected by your programs. They are the key informants in an evaluation.

CHAPTER EIGHT

Be Generous
and Raise Money

⊷⊶⊷⊶⊷

*We make a living by what we get, but we make a life by what
we give.*

— Winston Churchill

Nonprofit leaders are often exhausted by the struggle to raise
funds. But, in my experience, raising money, though very hard
work, can be empowering and satisfying. We are all both givers and
receivers on a daily basis. Similarly, at The Global Fund we were
both grant makers and grant seekers. We needed to raise money in
order to do our work, and our work was giving money away. The
way both processes were followed was crucial. In fact, the medium
was the message: we deeply believed that *how* we raised and donated money was as important, if not more important, than the
money itself. In this aspect of our work, as in every other, we
sought a new paradigm.

It cannot be denied that money is an awkward topic for many people. On the one hand, we hear people say, "Money makes the world go round" or "Money is power." On the other hand, we hear that "Money is the root of all evil," "Money cannot buy happiness," or "They're rich, but we're happy!" Perhaps all of these thoughts are true in some sense. But our conflicting views about money may hold us back from going out and getting it — in order to implement the programs that we think are important, as we try to change the world in positive ways.

Yes, money is a difficult subject, but there is money out there somewhere, and we who are concerned about changing the world in positive ways need it to carry out our worthy programs. This chapter contains some thoughts and tips about how to not only begin to raise funds but to enjoy doing it.

When we started The Global Fund for Women, I initially thought that we were raising money for one simple and straightforward reason: we were raising money for our program; we were raising money so we could give it away to women's groups around the world. But over time, raising money and working with donors revealed itself to be much more multifaceted and every bit as interesting as giving the funds away. We made what we were learning part of our program. We began to speak of and think of "donor activists" and of blurring the distinctions between givers and receivers. We began to see that money, like leadership and power, grows when you give it away. Donors began to feel connected with The Global Fund and to initiate programs themselves. We weren't simply raising money to support our programs. *We were offering people the opportunity to be giving, to be included, to have meaning in their lives.* It became increasingly obvious over the years that by encouraging people to be more giving we were offering them empowerment and a sense of connection and inclusion.

My lessons in fund-raising began when I was on the other side of the table, at the William and Flora Hewlett Foundation. I remember that back in the late 1970s I was visited by Jim Morgan, the then–executive director of World Neighbors, an international development organization. When I told him that I knew very little about his organization, he responded with excitement, saying that he wanted me to know more about World Neighbors, of which he was very proud. He stated up front that he felt that I would be excited and inspired by the work of the organization and that he wanted me to have the chance to be part of it. I thought at the time that he was not only a thoughtful person who truly believed in the work of his organization but also a very good fund-raiser.

When I began to raise funds for The Global Fund for Women, I believed that the idea of The Global Fund was so appealing that everyone who heard about it would immediately write a check to support it. However, after a friend who had not donated to The Global Fund said, "But you never asked me!" I quickly learned that it is vital to ask for money if you want to receive it. Asking is empowering and very satisfying, particularly when you have the ingenuity to figure out who and how best to ask. However, talking about, let alone asking for, money is very difficult for many people, especially in some cultures and especially for many women. But you can get past these difficulties if you are clear about the worth of your endeavor, project, or organization.

I have found that it is not possible to ask for money sincerely and openly unless some other tasks (those we have explored in previous chapters) have been considered and addressed. Before you begin fund-raising in earnest, make sure that you take care of these key tasks:

- Clarify your vision: What problem are you trying to address and how will you go about setting your program in place? Why are you creating the organization or project?

- Clarify your values: What do you stand for? What do you believe in?

- Clarify the roles of the various people involved: What kinds of people will be on the governing board or the advisory council? What kinds of staff persons will you invite to join you? Who will take leadership to speak for the organization? What processes will you follow to make decisions?

- Put in place a logical and clear system of managing money so that as you are able to raise funds, you can be accountable to those who give to your cause.

If you can approach a potential funder (an individual, a foundation, a corporation, a government agency, or a community agency) with the solid knowledge that your cause makes sense and your organization (however small, nascent, and modest it may be) is well managed and accountable, you will feel comfortable, confident, and empowered to ask. I always thought that this was what Gandhi meant when he said, "If the cause is right, the means will come."[1] This became my fund-raising mantra. As our budget rose over the years, I would sometimes wake up at night and wonder how in the world I could raise $1,000 a day, $2,000 a day, and so on. Then I would simply chant, "If the cause is right, the means will come." Somehow it helped.

A very important caution: I have learned that when people are in the business of raising money (or when they feel desperate for money), they can be tempted to bend the truth a little — to listen to a potential funder and suddenly find that they can cut, paste, squeeze, or otherwise amend their program to fit the funder's agenda. Do not do this! Learn from donors. Exemplify your principles of listening and connecting, and always consider the donors' ideas and views. But never go for the money as your first priority. Stay flexible and, most important, stay true to your vision. I have seen many organizations get caught on the slippery slope of trying to satisfy the interests of funders, thereby losing themselves and their own unique vision. Again, I am not advocating inflexibility; rather, I am trying to emphasize clarity.

I offer the following anecdote as an example of how easy it can be to dilute the vision of a program or an organization. Once, when we had decided to try to raise money by direct mail and had received some foundation support to do this, we turned to a very well-known consulting firm to help us prepare the materials, including the "ask" letter, and to run the campaign. Many people had told us that it was important to seek this kind of advice to ensure a maximum return. I discussed the concept, programs, and principles of The Fund at length with the consultant, and a week or two later, he sent the "ask" letter to me for my review.

The letter was shocking. It presented women as being needy victims of poverty and violence. It used militaristic terms throughout, depicting women as "targets" and empowerment as "a weapon in the battle for equality." The tone and the words were aggressive; they portrayed women as being at the mercy of forces beyond their control, rather than as independent people who, when given the chance, could change their circumstances. While we had decided early on that The Fund would always present women as strong and powerful in the face of tremendous difficulties, I was often told by fund-raising experts that to raise money we would have to tug at the hearts of potential donors by depicting women as battered, miserable victims. Against such advice, I revised the letter to follow my initial instincts about emphasizing women's strengths. The outcome of the test mailing was inconclusive, and we will never know whether going the other route (depicting women as miserable victims) would have raised more money. From then on, we wrote all of our own letters, describing women and their strengths and needs in terms of our vision. At least we were consistent, and we ultimately raised a lot of money.

Clarity of vision and consistency of principles are vitally important in fund-raising. In case after case at The Global Fund, I observed women's groups that were determined to change their societies; they were committed and driven. They worked hard to hone their vision and to create plans for implementing their vision that were integrated, balanced, and sensible. The groups that were most effective were those whose visions were clear.

In addition to clarifying the vision, the values, the structure, and the plan for your overall organization, you will want to tackle these same tasks with regard to your fund-raising program. More specifically, you will want to do the following:

- Align the vision, values, and goals of your fund-raising program with the vision, values, and goals of your organization.

- Develop a clear and logical plan for achieving specific goals, demonstrating your values, and realizing your vision.

- Determine how much the program will cost and how funds will be managed, and make a commitment to excellent management and clear reporting procedures.

- Make a commitment to diversity in fund-raising. Through diversity one learns about and is able to gain access to different groups of people and different funding sources. All activities are enhanced through diversity, and a fund-raising plan must include goals for obtaining funding from several difference sources: service clubs, members, income-producing activities, foundations, corporations, bake sales, government funders, et cetera.

- Make a commitment to treating all parts of your organization, including your donors, with equal respect and trust. This is a very important aspect of fund-raising. The board, advisors, and staff of an organization are important. So are the clients to whom a service is being provided. And equally important are the donors and potential donors. An organization seeking money is best seen as creating a partnership between a community of need and a community with resources.

After doing all of this, you can *ask for money*! And then, of course, after asking and receiving, you must *thank those who gave*. (I learned this from my mother's early training; in my childhood home, part of the day after Christmas was always spent writing our thank-you notes.)

Close on the heels of the letter or phone call to thank people is the next step: it is only courteous and strategic to *include these generous people in your work.* Including the donors means asking them how they would like to be involved beyond money. Would they like to learn more about the cause? Would they like to volunteer? Would they like to be invited to events and related programs? Would they like to help raise money? How would they like to be included?

What do you do after that? Thank your donors again, ask again; thank, include, thank, ask, include, and so on.

All of this requires excellent organization and very good databases, which are quite possible, especially now that we have the benefit of computers. One of my early mentors in fund-raising was Susan Hester, who worked with me in the fall of 1987 to help with initial fund-raising for The Global Fund. Coaching me to call and follow up on every lead, teaching me how to develop a list of prospects and to ask for money, never letting a detail of information get lost, Susan taught me the basics of fund-raising. From there, we created the base for the early operations of our organization. We raised about $150,000 in the first year and about $375,000 in the second, mostly from individual donors. Susan and I spoke by phone every day or two. She would counsel me, and I would follow her instructions. For example, she began by working with me to put together a list of potential donors, then she told me to set a timetable to call or meet with them to ask them for money, and then she followed up to make sure I had done this: "Have you called Mrs. X? Have you thanked Mr. Y? When are you going to do it? A week has gone by. Do it today. Finish your list by the end of this week. I'll call you on Friday to check up."

In some ways, all of this work was grueling. On the other hand, I loved the promise of The Global Fund and wanted people to be part of it. When they said, "Yes, I'll give," it was great! Fundraising gives fairly immediate rewards; when people say yes, it feels good. Remember: if someone says yes to your request, that is the very time when you must immediately make another call or have another meeting. The happiness in your voice will be infectious, and your next potential donor will react to it, usually positively, wanting to be part of a positive experience. Keep in mind, too, that about 50 percent of the time when you ask for money face to face, you will be turned down. But that means that 50 percent of the time you will succeed! You *will* raise money if you ask enough people. Ask a homeless person on a street corner to confirm this; if they ask enough people, they raise money. (They have a very hard fund-raising job; be among the 50 percent of people who give to them.)

Raising Money from Individual People

When you begin a group or an important project — perhaps you have just an idea and two or three other people at that point — you may need a relatively small amount of money. I believe strongly that much positive change can occur in the world when a small group of people determines to implement a vision. So I encourage you to take your vision, devise a plan, and begin. Raise a small amount of money to register your new group, get some printed letterhead paper, and hold a planning meeting. Or you might decide to send one of your colleagues to a conference or a meeting. Or you might set in place a membership campaign. Each of these activities will cost relatively little money. Of course, you may eventually need more resources to implement your long-range plan and realize your vision.

Here are some proven ways to raise money:

- Be a donor yourself. This is the easiest way to raise money, if it is possible. It is freeing and empowering to give, and if you are not willing to financially support the effort (even in a very small way), why should anyone else do so?

- Ask your friends to become donors. List all of your friends who are interested in your event or project. Decide how much you think each of them can afford to donate, then write to them personally, include a description of your activity and why it is important that this activity happen, and ask them to support you. Visit or phone those who do not respond within two weeks. If you are trying to raise $1,000, for example, you will need ten friends who could give $100 each, twenty friends who can give $50 each, or forty who can give $25 each. If you explain why the activity is important and what higher good will come from it, and if you have donated money to it yourself, it will be easy to ask.

- Ask friends to match your donation. Give part of the total that you are trying to raise, and ask your friends to add to your donation for a total of $1,000. This is very effective because you are not asking them to do anything you haven't done.

- Host an informal party or a tea party. Invite as many people as you know. Pause during the festivities to talk about your effort, vision, and plan. Ask people to do-nate between $20 and $50 toward your activity. Leave a basket by the door, point it out, and let people know exactly how you will use their donations.

- Organize dinner parties. With two or three friends, meet for a simple — and delicious — dinner during which you discuss your program goals. Do this with as many people as you know and ask them to donate $20 each. Again, explain to them how you will use the proceeds.

- Make a list of the businesses, religious institutions, and clubs you know of in your community. Make an appointment with the head of each and explain why it is important that your activity happen. Ask for a donation and offer to give a talk to their staff or members when the activity takes place or is finished.

- Find a spokesperson. Get a well-known and popular person in your community to do a special event; ask a friend to host it in her home. Charge people $50 for the event, describing the worthy cause to which you will direct the money.

- Start a chain dinner. Invite twelve people to a dinner and charge them $20 each. Get two people of the twelve at your dinner to invite twelve other people to dinner and charge those people $20 each. Then have two people from each of those two dinners host twelve people at $20 each, and so on. You can use any dollar amount or number of diners, and your friends will like the idea of helping you start your planned activity.

One or a combination of any of these methods will raise money. After your successful fund-raising efforts, remember to thank all of the people who made a donation, and then go ahead and thank them again. When your planned program or activity gets under way, invite your supporters to a modest gathering, tell them about the success of the activity at that point, and restate why the activity is important. Thank them again. Ask them if they would like to be more active in the venture. They have now become part of your group; they share your vision and are now a tangible part of your network of empowerment.

⋘⋙

So far I have been writing about raising relatively small amounts of money from individual people. If that is what you plan to do, I strongly urge you to try to raise the money within your own community, however you may define that term. Go where the money is. When Willie Sutton, a famous bank robber, was asked, "Why do you rob banks?" he answered, "Because that is where the money is!"[2] While I do not advise you to rob banks, I do encourage you to think about all of the events and situations when people exchange or give money: on birthdays, weddings, or anniversaries; as tips, payments for services or products, or bequests; in wills; for membership dues; et cetera. Use your imagination and think about how your organization can engage people at those times or in those places in order to provide funds for your worthy cause.

At The Global Fund, once we got into the swing of fundraising, wonderful stories of the generosity of individuals became frequent. People honored others on their birthdays or weddings by giving a donation to The Global Fund in the honoree's name. A resource network of businesswomen developed, and these women instituted their own fund-raising efforts for us. Individual donors created funds and encouraged their friends to give to The Global Fund. A study circle of donors came together to study trafficking in women and to give donations to groups working on that issue. A physician accepted payment from some clients in the form of donations to The Global Fund. Children raised money on our behalf on the occasion of their graduations or their bat mitzvahs. It was all very exciting.

Although many of these experiences were unexpected — they were initiated by individuals outside of the organization who were excited by the vision of The Global Fund — they were also planned, in the sense that we tried to involve people and challenge them to work with us, to help us. And we kept track of all of this in our expanding and efficient databases.

You might want to keep in mind the fund-raising advice of Benjamin Franklin. When he was asked how to raise money for a new meeting house, he replied, "In the first place, I advise you to apply to all those who you know will give something; next to those of whom you are uncertain whether they will give anything or not, and show them the list of those who have given; and lastly, do not neglect those who you are sure will give nothing; for in some of them you may be mistaken."[3] Franklin was suggesting that you ask everyone for support. In some ways, I agree; everyone is a potential giver, and people want to be generous. However, I also disagree with Franklin to some extent, partly because of some more advice that I received from Bill Hewlett.

Early on in my efforts to raise money for The Global Fund, I paid a visit to Bill to ask him for a very large donation. His response was not what I wanted, but his words stayed with me. Bill told me that he didn't give the kind of money I was requesting for issues that "didn't keep him awake at night." Environmental degradation and population growth kept him awake at night, he told me, but the difficulties of women in the world were not his thing, not an issue he felt strongly about. He said that he did care, but that women's issues were not at the center of his feelings. He would support my effort, he said, but not in a major way. I remember saying to him that people like him ought to be kept awake at night by the unfair situation of women and that women's rights issues related to some of his stated interests. He responded by reiterating that he supported other worthy causes and that what I needed to do was to go and find the people who *were* kept awake at night by their concern for women and women's issues. Find the right people for your cause, he urged.

I realized the importance of what Bill was telling me. I realized that I didn't have to get money from everybody to make The Global Fund work. I did not have to waste precious time and energy beating my head against the proverbial wall trying to convince people to send money our way, toward Global Fund issues, when that was not what ignited their passion. I learned that there are a lot of generous and wonderful donors whose priorities and interests differ from mine. My job was to find and focus on those who were willing to learn about and possibly share my priority — a deep commitment to women's issues. I needed to find people who would find meaning in their lives by being included in our exciting enterprise.

In other words, you need to find out what motivates people to give to one cause rather than another. You can learn much from the donors themselves. Ask them to help you understand their motivations. I spoke at length with our donors about why they cared so much about our work. Several of the businesswomen told me that working with The Global Fund made them feel connected to women around the world and that helping women become more empowered made them feel relevant; it gave meaning to their lives.

In my roles as fund-raiser and president of The Global Fund, I was often asked why men should support women's empowerment. Why should men become donors to an organization that is dedicated to empowering women, to making women's rights human rights, and to creating a world in which women's efforts are recognized and valued? Should men give up power to make way for women? What's in it for men if women become fully equal?

In order to get some answers, I decided to go to the source: I asked some men who had supported The Global Fund to talk about why they had done so. One donor who provided major funding to our organization told me he specifically liked the fact that we focused on partnership between men and women rather than on polarization. He liked the *how* of what we did — linking with anyone who cared about our issues and valuing each other — more than the *what*. Another supporter of The Fund stated that empowering women was "the right thing to do." He went on to say that it made him feel good to "do the right thing." He also believed that the absence of women in his workplace, a major Silicon Valley corporation, had led to less imagination and less creativity. He considered himself a feminist, in the sense that he believed that all people should treat each other with kindness and consideration and that the structures of society needed to be changed to address the harm that current structures had done to both women and men.

Another man expressed the view that supporting women made him recognize his own full humanity and that a partnership between men and women was the wave of the future. He did not want to be left out of a trend toward equality. Yet another male donor believed that the world needs women in leadership roles. It needs women's talents and wisdom. He felt that the world needs women's experience of not only surviving but of rising above adversity, poverty, and violence and continuing to be loving, caring, nurturing people. The world needs this particular kind of wisdom, he thought, and men need the example of women.

It was fascinating to speak with these people who had supported The Global Fund. Their rationales for giving helped me tremendously as I approached other people for support. I learned from their different perspectives, as you will learn if you speak directly and listen to those who support your vision and your program.

Raising Money from Institutions

So far, we have been discussing raising money from individuals; I believe that having a strong individual donor base is very important, not only for sustaining an organization but also for learning from many different people. But you may wish to diversify your fund-raising, or you may need to raise significant amounts of money that may only be available from larger, institutional funders, such as corporations and foundations.

At The Global Fund we didn't have very much luck raising money from corporations. We learned that, for the most part, they wanted to give to local rather than international causes (local arts organizations, schools, or girls' and boys' clubs). They had two primary motivations for giving money: they wanted to be seen as good community citizens, and they wanted to respond to the interests of their own employees — both worthy goals. Nevertheless, we did try to raise money from local corporations, particularly those that worked internationally, and we had mixed success. More successful were our efforts with local businesses, since we were able to connect with individual business owners and draw them into our work. Our approach with small business owners was to ask them to give a small percentage of their profits to The Global Fund on one particular day, International Women's Day, March 8, for example. If your program or group is local, approach local businesses (the bank, a department store, a restaurant) and partner with them for the betterment of your community.

In contrast, we were very successful at raising money for The Global Fund from foundations. At the beginning, this was partly because I had come out of that world and knew a lot of people in foundations who were interested in international work. But we were successful also because we carefully analyzed the interests of many foundations and chose to approach those where we could see a clear connection between their visions and agendas and ours.

There is no magic involved in obtaining money from foundations; it involves hard and steady work as well as clarity about your purposes and programs. But before you write to potential institutional funders, keep in mind some of the following thoughts:

- Remember that applying for money goes far beyond writing a proposal. Your organization's management and financial systems, however modest, must be in excellent order, so that you can express clearly what you do, how you do it, and why you do it.

- Try to learn more about the funding agency, including asking for an annual report or program description and finding out the name of the appropriate person to write to when applying for a grant.

- Read the agency's annual report and grant guidelines very carefully and decide whether the vision, mission, and goals of the funding agency fit with your group's activities and goals. If they do, write a letter of inquiry or a proposal, following the agency's application guidelines. If they do not, don't waste your time and theirs by applying.

• Have a clear idea of your fund-raising goals so that you can tell the foundation representative how a donation from their organization will fit with your general plans for fund-raising. (In other words, have a fund-raising plan.)

• After you have written and submitted a letter of inquiry or a proposal, follow up within a week or two to make sure that the organization received your request. Try to establish a relationship with the contact person. Treat her or him as a partner. Often when I met a foundation representative who seemed very interested in our work but who could not get his or her foundation to provide funds to The Global Fund, I would ask that person for an individual donation. Bringing such a person into your circle can be a gift to her or him; it also expands your network of interested people and may even lead you to other sources of support.

• Keep in mind that foundations and other agencies turn down some 90 percent of the proposals they receive. If you are turned down, don't feel bad or rejected. Write a nice letter thanking the funder for her or his time. Even if you have been turned down, your good relationship with the potential donor will expand your network.

- If you receive a grant, thank the donor soon. Stay in regular contact, and be prompt about sending back necessary documents and reports.

- Always meet deadlines. If you cannot send a report on time, write to explain why.

- Don't be shy about asking for funds again. Discuss with your contact person the best approach and timing for requesting another grant. Share your hopes and dreams with her or him.

- Most important, always remember that people at funding agencies are human beings. They care about good causes. If they are treated just as a source of money, they will feel bad. They want and need to be treated with warmth and respect. And some of them are interested in becoming donors themselves.

Raising money beyond your own community — from foundations or other institutional donors — has costs as well as benefits. On the one hand, you may gain money for your worthy cause. On the other hand, even when people try hard to create a relationship of equality between donors and recipients, money can represent power, and a relationship based on money can accentuate existing differences between people. This may be especially true if you are obtaining funding from large institutions, such as foundations or multilateral agencies, which may have their own very clear agendas. It can sometimes be difficult to maintain freedom and independence in the face of large amounts of money. For this reason, I emphasize a diverse fundraising approach, without dependence on only one or two major sources of funding.

Sharing Fund-raising Skills

Although The Global Fund did not generally provide technical assistance to women's groups, over the years many women from the groups that we had supported asked us to share our knowledge and experience of fund-raising. As a result, I wrote a modest guide to fund-raising (from which I have drawn in writing this chapter). We also put together a series of fund-raising workshops and offered them at regional meetings around the world (in Africa, Asia, and Latin America), hoping to train people to use our materials and do the teaching. This worked, and at the time of the Fourth World Conference on Women, held in 1995 in Beijing, China, at the concurrent Non-Governmental Forum we were able to present fund-raising workshops in five languages (Chinese, English, French, Russian, and Spanish), led by women who had been in our workshops at the regional meetings preceding the Beijing meeting. Also, our annual reports included outlines for a basic proposal for funding and a final report assessing the impact of a grant; these outlines laid out several basic questions for grantees to follow. We knew we were dealing with women who may not have had experience in applying outside of their own communities for funds, and we felt that these documents would help them organize their thoughts and effectively approach institutional donors and raise money.

I remember several occasions at the fund-raising workshops when women would exclaim, "I get it! Fund-raising can be fun!" They had suddenly realized that it was exhilarating to reach out to people, to share their excitement about their important work, and to offer people the chance to be involved. Fund-raising is not begging. People raising money for their worthy causes are not supplicants. They are honest and enthusiastic people who have the drive to share their excitement about making positive change as well as the willingness to widen their vision and their plans to include many other people.

I know that many of the women's groups that were funded through The Global Fund were started and sustained by women who were going to do what they were doing anyway — with or without our funding or anybody else's. The women in Korea concerned about violence against women, the lawyers in southern Africa creating networks to promote legal literacy among women, the workers in Nigeria providing health care in small villages, all had come together to help others before The Global Fund had arrived on the scene. Similarly, I was so driven by my desire to realize The Global Fund that I probably would have persisted in some fashion without major help. But our grants *did* help others, just as The Fund was helped by its donors.

The Global Fund grants encouraged remarkable women; they made them feel valued; they connected them to a wider network. Over and over, women's groups told us that our grants gave them the additional empowerment or belief in themselves that allowed them to do and be more. The stories of their work to effect legislation, offer services to women suffering abuse, challenge inheritance laws, and just bring women together to share there experiences empowered us in turn. Keep this in mind when you are a donor yourself. Giving money away empowers both the giver and the receiver.

I felt the same way when donations arrived at our office. The money was important, but the encouragement and goodwill that came with the money were truly empowering. Money does not make the world go round, and no, it cannot buy happiness, but it is useful, and it can be a tool for connection. The giver-receiver connection brings together people who share dreams of a better world for all.

Things to Remember
as You Cultivate Your Dreams

- Be clear about what you are doing and why.

- Set in place excellent management systems, including superb databases and a fund-raising plan.

- As leader and manager, your primary responsibilities are to articulate the vision and raise the money.

- Ask for what you want and be able to defend your request.

- Thank and include those who give. Ask, thank, and include.

- Treat donors in an evenhanded way. A gift of any size is an expression of generosity and love; disdain no gift, however small it may be.

- Be a financial donor yourself and observe what you receive by giving.

- Most important: know that when you raise funds, you are offering people a connection to your good work. You are expanding their world by inviting them to join you. And you are strengthening yourself by having them share your dreams.

CHAPTER NINE

Lead and Share Leadership

⸻⸻ ⚬⚬⚬⚬⚬⚬⚬ ⸻⸻

Go to the people
Learn from them
Love them
Start with what they know
Build on what they have
But of the best leaders
When their task is accomplished
Their work is done
The people will remark:
"We have done it ourselves."

— Lao Tzu

In my view, outstanding leadership is characterized by learning from others and sharing and giving away power. An example of this type of leadership is seen in Tewa, an organization in Nepal that provides funds to small women's groups in rural parts of that country. Rita Thapa, a former grantee and board member of The Global Fund for Women, was inspired in a workshop of The Global Fund at the 1995 Beijing meeting to create a new organization. Based on her experience of doing development work in Nepal for over a decade, she observed, adapted, and went beyond The Global Fund model when she founded Tewa, which means "support" in Nepali. She drew together a very diverse group of Nepali women from different castes and ethnicities. They created an organization that not only made grants to registered women's organizations in rural Nepal but also welcomed the financial and intellectual support of individual people within such groups. At the same time, Tewa fund-raised successfully in a country where asking local people directly for money to support efforts to strengthen women was completely new. The women of Tewa reached out to rich and poor alike, including them as donors, volunteers, and workers. Leadership was shared from the beginning. The transition from the founding leadership happened after less than six years and was smooth and apparently seamless. The organization continues to thrive, having acquired land and built five buildings so far, including the Tewa office building. Consistently fostering the values expressed in its processes and structures in a conflict-ridden Nepal, Tewa is successfully integrating development, environment, and culture through its land and building development project and at the same time ensuring Tewa's sustainability in a deteriorating economic climate.

Another example of shared leadership in action took place when some women in Southeast Asia suggested that The Global Fund hold a meeting of grantees and advisors in the region. We turned to one of the grantee groups in the Philippines and invited them to take the lead. They collaborated fully with the groups in the region to identify an appropriate format and locale and to outline an agenda. A woman's group in Singapore hosted the meeting. We wanted the participating groups to feel comfortable talking among themselves, and so we wanted them to determine for themselves whether to include people, particularly donors like us, from outside the region. We were flattered to be invited to participate when the meeting took place in late 1992.

This Singapore meeting was like none that I had attended before. It was full of flowers and open conversations, and it was both restful and exciting. Two women from The Fund participated, but they did not direct the meeting in any way. The women in attendance resolved to work together to create a network to focus on issues of sex trafficking in the region of Southeast Asia. The work grew to include numerous groups and networks, as well as a project that involved advisors, donors, and grantees who learned about and initiated efforts in other regions to prevent the trafficking of women and girls.

Both the work of Tewa in Nepal and the meeting of advisors and grantees in Singapore are only two of many groups that epitomized our values of inclusion, transparency, respect, and compassion. They also focused on moving forward and taking responsibility to get a job done. They exemplify what I view as effective leadership, the subject that we explore in this chapter.

Defining Leadership

What is leadership? Is it people getting to the top? Is it people becoming famous? Often, the concept of leadership is articulated as the special qualities or abilities an individual possesses or as what a leader does. When asked to define leadership, people tend to respond by describing an individual person, a leader. This tendency to see leadership only in terms of the people who have made it to the top has been a comfortable model in the United States, where a single leader in a high position is an expression of individualism. But true leadership, I believe, is an expression of a more communal approach, in which people at all levels of society and in organizations imagine positive change and begin to take responsibility for changing themselves and their communities.

In my eyes, then, leadership begins with people actively and consciously taking on responsibility to make things happen. By carrying out that responsibility within the context of a program or organization, a person increases her or his influence within the program or group. Think of your own experiences: if you want to have more influence in a meeting or in a group, the thing to do is to participate, to take on responsibility. I have noticed in various board meetings, for example, that people who volunteer to take notes and produce minutes end up having influence over the direction of the organization. People who take on the responsibility of being on a nominating committee can end up wielding influence over the composition of a group or an organization. Individuals who volunteer to organize or chair a meeting and carry through with that responsibility also expand their leadership abilities and influence.

In the course of my years at The Global Fund, my idea of leadership grew to include the following elements: having the capacity and willingness to articulate a vision for change, feeling able and willing to develop and implement a plan to work toward attaining the vision, and drawing together many different kinds of people, including them, and learning from them to work toward the vision.

Developing a New Paradigm for Leadership

Generally when people think of leadership, they imagine a kind of hierarchy, and it is true that leadership implies taking on greater responsibility and therefore having more influence and possibly more power than others. How do we reconcile this suggestion of hierarchy with our desire for a different kind of paradigm in social relationships? Some people argue that new styles of leadership are necessary for successful progress, styles that emphasize shared responsibility and power, cooperation, and inclusiveness, and I agree. Leadership for the future, I believe, has a great deal to do with having a vision that can be shared and then working with many different people to bring about that vision.

The leaders who have gone before us — the giants of industry, the political leaders, and the well-known figures of the past, who are mostly older, white, and male — might argue that they made successful progress without demonstrating this sharing of power, this collaboration, this inclusiveness. But is that model of hierarchy and command and control, whether exhibited by men or women, appropriate to our time and needs? Leadership in that old sense — authority, control, superiority, and being first and foremost — has been a successful strategy until recently. Organizations have been built around this kind of leadership, where one person rises to the top and others follow. Charismatic leaders have led movements, and others have felt honored to be followers. But given the changes in our world, this type of one-person leadership seems inappropriate. The problems that will face us over the next few decades demand a different approach to leadership. In our globalized world, we need as many people as possible to feel able to dream of positive change and to take responsibility for some of that change.

At The Global Fund, leadership emerged from many different places within the organization as more people shared the vision and began to take responsibility to make things happen. We attempted to eliminate hierarchy, but we insisted on accountability and various loci of responsibility. Teams, as we have seen, were a part of this. As leaders appeared among staff, donors, and volunteers or among grantees, we viewed them as managers or facilitators, rather than as heads of hierarchies who felt they must be in control, with people under them. (Titles are important, I think, and we preferred *manager* to *director* for staff team leaders.) These leaders consciously returned to the vision and the values on which our work was based, thus providing a sense of clear context in which those around them could work.

Sharing leadership also means sharing the public face of an organization or campaign, which results in greater strength for the cause over time. I believe that it is much more effective for an organization or a group to exhibit and be seen to exhibit shared leadership rather than to promote one person as the sole leader or only face of the organization. Certainly, as I have noted before, I believe it is necessary to have one person be responsible for the overall health of the organization. But as the vision, goals, and programs of your organization or project are expressed, I would urge you to have many people serve as the spokespersons for your cause. By consciously asking many different staff people, board members, or others to represent The Fund at meetings, particularly the meetings preceding the 1995 Beijing women's conference, I hoped to have the "face" of The Global Fund be many faces. By having different people sign letters and other communications emanating from The Global Fund, we hoped to reflect the reality of The Fund being a place where vision and work were shared by many.

Promoting Women in Leadership

Some people argue that the new styles of leadership emphasizing shared responsibility and power, cooperation, and inclusiveness have been identified with women in particular. Why would this be? Could it be that taking on responsibility comes more easily to women, who have been expected to fulfill the traditional roles of mother and nurturer (being responsible for producing the next generation)?

At a conference on women's leadership at Mills College in June 1993, Dame Nita Barrow, the convener of the Non-Governmental Forum on Women held in Nairobi in 1985 and a member of the board of The Global Fund for Women, offered this definition of leadership, which she credited to Henry Kissinger: "Leadership is getting a hundred little things done a little better." She noted that women might be particularly well suited to this sort of leadership, not only because we are well equipped to appreciate the small, human aspects of life but because, by dint of our position as the majority of the poor, we may have special skills to address the effects of disintegration and deprivation, tasks that Dame Nita saw as the challenge of the next decades.

I would not argue that women have a corner on this different kind of leadership. However, because of our experiences we may be more attuned to leadership that requires creating community and forging relationships. Carol Gilligan identified the "different voice" that women are more likely to bring to problem solving — an approach that views the person as part of a web of relationships rather than standing apart.[1] This approach seems appropriate to addressing the kinds of problems we face today. With our particular perspectives and life experiences, women have seen the value of community, pluralism, kindness, and caring. This may give us the strength to fully participate in the responsibilities of leadership in the world. We need to use this capacity to its limits for our own sakes and for the sake of humanity. Such leadership and competence are essential for positive social change to occur around the world.

That women would even contemplate leading is remarkable

to me, given the number of obstacles to overcome in order to participate fully in society: lack of day care and health care, violence, prejudice, inequality, and lack of financial resources, to name a few. Yet the number of women's groups around the world continues to grow, and the number of women leading has greatly increased over the years. By the sixth year of The Global Fund, we had supported more than four hundred groups, and we had observed more and more women emerging as positional leaders, as heads of not-for-profit and for-profit groups and even as leaders in governments. It was clear to me that the increased development and support of women's groups and the emergence of new women leaders were linked. I came to see leadership as being directly related to empowerment.

Some of the women who have emerged as positional leaders — in the Philippines and Pakistan, for example, and as heads of corporations and other organizations — have ridden in on their husbands' or their fathers' names. Some of these positional leaders shared the party and platform of the men that preceded them. And some, in Chile, Germany, and Liberia, for example, have emerged on their own. These women have all taken on responsibility and become leaders, and they have been selected and described as such. But in a good number of cases, these leaders have followed old styles of leadership, based on command, control, and rigid hierarchy. However, I would argue that they are the minority, and that most of the women and some of the men emerging as leaders today believe strongly in learning from, supporting, and valuing each other and other people rather than achieving alone.

Again and again, in conferences of women discussing leadership, that point — the need for people (and particularly women) to value each other — is highlighted, as women share their sense of being left out, of being mistrusted, of being unsupported, even by women and perhaps particularly by women who may be different from themselves in terms of sexual preference, disability, race, age, class, et cetera. I cannot overemphasize the importance of thinking of leadership not as superiority, dominance, and going first, but as supporting each other, valuing one another, and sharing responsibility, ideas, and decision making.

Among the hundreds of women's groups The Global Fund partnered with we saw leadership in the new, communal sense. As I have described, these groups usually begin with three or four women coming together, deciding that a problem needs to be addressed, and exercising the capacity, energy, and skills to embark on work toward their shared vision (in other words, taking responsibility for change). They then seek to draw other people into their vision, partnering with them and learning from their talents and resources to work for change. They recognize that their vision will be realized and true change will come only when that vision is shared by all. These women see leadership as an exercise in democratic values. Their brand of leadership is enhanced by sharing it, giving it away.

Another outstanding example of shared leadership and principles-based management is the African Women's Development Fund (AWDF), originally conceived at a planning meeting in 1995 supported by The Global Fund. The AWDF was formally established in 2000 by a small group of women to support the work of women's groups so that African women can live "in a changed world with integrity and in peace." The website of the AWDF is dear to my heart. Open it up and you immediately recognize that many people participate in the work, share the vision, and contribute with diverse experiences. Especially impressive to me is the clear statement, very prominent on the website, of values and principles, which sets the tone for the work of this Africa-wide organization.[2]

In the approaches that women's groups are taking to the problems that they face, we see a demonstrated concern for others, particularly for the generations that will follow. We see inclusion and respect for others, as well as recognition that we can all learn from one another. We see an emphasis on community and communication. At The Global Fund we shared with women around the world a vision of a world in which people could be good to each other and at the same time do effective work by reaching out inclusively to involve people who were different one from another.

Women in places like Afghanistan, Iraq, the former Soviet Union, and South Africa are proclaiming that *there can be no democracy without women* even as they may be left out of current government structures. The support for the new leaders in Bolivia, Chile, and Liberia, which came from heretofore marginalized parts of the population, bode well for more inclusive structures of governance. And in the nonprofit sector, in organizations such as the African Women's Development Fund and Tewa, there are models of leadership and democracy designed by communities and characterized by diversity, respect, learning, and shared leadership. Women are proving to be up to the task of defining a new paradigm of leadership, as they come together to create group after group in the face of widespread disintegration and deprivation in an attempt to make positive change.

Over the years, we saw thousands of women's groups emerging around the world with visions of a different future for women and society. These women were no longer content to passively allow leadership that was often indecisive, lacking in vision, ineffective, devoid of compassion, and even corrupt to determine the quality and course of their lives. They were taking matters into their own hands, taking responsibility, working toward visions of a different future by leading in their own ways to effectively change their worlds.

Often, these groups were defining new roles as political alignments and patterns changed. Here are some examples of the many notable women's groups that formed because of new political and economic opportunities in the mid-1990s:

- In various parts of the world, women's groups worked to ensure that women's equality was addressed in legislation and in the formation of new constitutions. In Cameroon, for example, the International Federation of Women Lawyers focused on the passage of legislation that established women's equal rights to private property ownership, child custody, and inheritance. Similarly, the Mongolian Women Lawyers' Association was instrumental in ensuring that women's equality was addressed in the country's new constitution.

- In eastern Europe, groups such as Asociace Podnikatelek a Managerek, in the Czech Republic, and the International Federation of Business and Professional Women, in Albania, worked to strengthen women's initiatives in entrepreneurial activities and to open communication links among businesswomen.

- Other groups worked to increase direct participation in political and governance systems. The Society for the Advancement of Women in Malawi, for example, organized workshops on gender equality and the role of women in the country's political process. The

Jerusalem Link: A Women's Joint Venture for Peace, in Israel, worked across ethnic lines to empower women and assist them to participate in elections. The Centro Feminista de Estudos e Assessoria, a nonpartisan awareness-raising group in Brazil, provided access to information about the legislative process to a wide range of women's organizations. In India, the Women's Political Watch focused its activities on the election and appointment of women at significant levels in government. Finally, in South Africa, the Women's College coordinated leadership and management training programs for women within both the public and the private sectors.

Clearly, leadership was emerging in many places and from many levels of society, as women felt strong enough to take responsibility for change.

❦

At the time our eighth annual report went to press in September 1995, women were gathering in Beijing, China, for the Fourth World Conference on Women and the parallel nongovernmental organization forum. The 1995 Beijing meeting — or more accurately, the NGO meeting, held thirty kilometers from Beijing, in Hairou — provided the world with an example of shared leadership by women, as some thirty thousand women converged to express their visions for the future and to link with one another toward a better future. By raising funds specifically for the purpose, we gave every staff person at The Global Fund who wanted to attend the meeting the opportunity to do so. The meeting allowed all of us to join together on a grand scale with new leaders from around the globe. For me personally, the meeting served as a backdrop to my own drive to both share leadership and pass it on, as I explain in detail in chapter 10.

Sharing the New Paradigm

Although examples of this kind of shared, caring, and respectful leadership are very often seen among women's groups, the qualities of compassion and collaboration must become social factors in the society as a whole. It is vital that women's visions be understood and shared for the greater good. There may be many paths toward leadership and many ways that women and men may lead. But as promising models emerge, particularly from women's experiences, these must be exported from the women's movement into the wider society.

Each new day of work at The Global Fund, it seemed, presented us with evidence that equal partnership between men and women was critical to global health and harmony. We saw increasing evidence that both women and men were beginning to feel able to define their own needs and solutions. We saw that listening, learning, and sharing knowledge and experience — within and without the organization — were essential to attaining our mission. We saw that by learning from the most marginalized people we could gain insights necessary to change the systems that distorted the lives of men and women worldwide.

Over time at The Global Fund I became increasingly convinced that progressive, communal leadership is a key ingredient to positive social change. Other civil society organizations were also becoming interested in the centrality of leadership, examining how leaders emerge and how to encourage new models of leadership. For example, in a 1992 publication of the Independent Sector (a U.S.-based network of NGOs), I read: "Usually when we think of leaders and leadership, we envision the towering giant who can do anything or the charismatic magician who can get the rest of us to do anything...[but] Most leadership actually comes from ordinary people who have it in them and rise to responsibility. These people are all around us leading thousands of community and national institutions through conviction, hard work, and quiet ability."[3]

Indeed, anyone can be a leader; it is a latent quality within all of us that waits to emerge. Every person can pursue a vision, implement a plan toward that vision, be open to diversity, be inclusive, and welcome others to the shared vision. In such a way, all of us can find meaning by exercising leadership. An important way that we can make a major difference to the future is to demonstrate leadership within our own organizations to change the way our business is done. All of us can create systems and structures that stress the value of diversity, inclusiveness, collaboration, and caring.

If we are going to create a better world, we ourselves must be leaders. Our organizations and groups must exhibit leadership too, not just in our programs but in our processes and structures. I think of Vaclav Havel's belief, quoted in the prologue of this book, that the "modern age has ended" and that we are going through a period in which "It is as if something were crumbling, decaying, and exhausting itself, while something else, still indistinct, were arising from the rubble." The "something else," I believe, is the emergence of a different kind of leadership that will be effective in our troubling times because it is based on values of inclusion, respect, and compassion.

*Things to Remember
as You Cultivate Your Dreams*

- Learn from others and share a clear vision.

- Consciously take responsibility for positive change.

- Lead by welcoming and valuing diverse people who share your vision and by seeking and learning from their ideas.

- Know that leadership can emerge from any part of an organization or community.

- Lead with generosity and modesty.

- Define your ideal of leadership, then exhibit it, give it away, and welcome it from anywhere and everywhere.

- Don't be afraid to hand over leadership or responsibility.

- Remember that leadership is not about gaining power for one's own benefit but about being a vehicle to improve the world.

CHAPTER TEN

Plan and Know
When to Move On

───── ⟨◎∕◎∕◎∕◎∕◎◎⟩ ─────

Not in [her] goals but in [her] transitions [wo]man is great.

— Ralph Waldo Emerson

At the time that we at The Global Fund were anticipating the Fourth World Conference on Women, which was to be held in 1995 in Beijing, China, the weight of our work began to bear down on me. Each day was filled with phone calls that had to be answered, individual donors who had to be met, speeches that had to be given. Growing lists of requests, inquiries, and grants from around the world awaited our attention. The sheer numbers of these items — and the unmet need that the numbers represented — sometimes seemed overwhelming. The female human rights issues that we were dealing with were so widespread, so persistent, so vicious. Over time, I was becoming heavy rather than lighthearted, a fact that I struggled to ignore.

Each new day brought more requests from brave women wanting to connect with us. In the face of women organizing to work against bride burnings in India or AIDS in Botswana or rape in Kosovo, of women working to legalize abortion in Latin America or daring to be forthrightly feminist in countries governed by Islamic law, how could I give in to fatigue?

In early 1995, I gave a talk in front of a group of two hundred professional women in San Francisco, describing how important it was for The Global Fund to listen to the thoughts and dreams of women worldwide. I spoke of how honored we felt to learn from the women's groups that contacted us. I explained that we often referred to our assistance to women's groups as the heart of the work of The Global Fund and that we believed that combining heart and head was an effective way to make positive change. I closed my remarks with a reminder of the importance of listening to our hearts.

As I stood in front of the audience, I could see people eagerly nodding in agreement; they clearly had understood and even been moved by what I had said. But something I had not expected was happening to me. I found myself ever so slightly disinterested — in my own words. Meaningful as I thought the words were, I realized that I had said them too many times; the same old ideas were coming from my lips.

The historic world conference on women, in Beijing, would leave me similarly less affected than I had expected. While many colleagues found the meeting to be exhilarating and even life-changing, for me it was an interesting meeting that represented a huge expenditure of funds that might have been better used by individual organizations to strengthen and implement their programs at home. I had seen so much of this before: meetings touted to be momentous that produced few tangible results, documents drafted that sat on shelves. And while I believe in and support the United Nations, I had observed the subordination of women within it and well knew how slow it could be to act. Though the conference was the largest United Nations and international NGO gathering ever — and surely the largest gathering of women in history — viable and bold strategies for changing the world for women did not emerge clearly. What did emerge were hundreds of networks of women's groups around the world. But within the UN system itself, although goals were set, strategies for significant global change were not fully developed.

During the year leading up to the Beijing meeting, I had met with the conference organizers on several occasions and strongly urged them to work with us to call on friends in the high-technology industry to help make the conference the most modern, technologically speaking, ever. I thought that the proceedings should be available worldwide and that in this way women's potential to connect with one another and come up with strong plans for change would be greatly enhanced. Women unable to attend the meeting could be included. Further, I suggested that we create a vision statement for the conference; this idea was worked through in New York by a group of us, and parts of the idea made their way into the final documents for the meeting. As it turned out, my hope for what the Beijing event might have offered may have been too ambitious or simply too much work. In any case, it didn't happen, and the meeting left me a bit flat. Looking back, ten years later, I am sad that those monitoring the long-term gains from the Beijing Platform of Action have come to believe that governments worldwide have not fulfilled most of the promises they made in Beijing. (The title of a report issued in 2005 by the Women's Environment and Development Organization — *Beijing Betrayed* — is sadly revealing.) Still, there is no doubt that I was tired back in 1995. Surely I must have been very tired not to have been fundamentally moved by what was without question such an extraordinary global event as that conference in China.

There were other reasons for fatigue. I think of Khunying Kanita, a Thai woman who attended the Singapore workshop that I mentioned in the previous chapter. When asked why she had come to that meeting, Kanita said, "Twelve years ago, there were twelve-year-olds being sold into prostitution. Now there are more of them. I have worked for twelve years. I am tired; I came to rest." The other women in attendance nodded their heads in recognition — not of hopelessness, but of exhaustion. They needed to sleep, to rest, to retreat from the hard work, the violence, the injustice.

It was more than just the volume and intensity of the work; it was the nature of the work that had caused my heart to seek refuge. I needed to recover, I think, from the pain of hearing women tell what was happening to us: the violence, the deprivation, the cruel practices rooted in centuries of tradition, the economic and social subordination. The utter pain and injustice of it all! This is why burnout is common among those who work to effect positive change against entrenched forces, and especially common, I think, among those who work on human rights issues.

Weariness and worry that my words were becoming rote were not the only clues that led me to think of moving on from The Global Fund. I found myself wanting to take time to read, to walk on beaches, to take up the guitar again. When I started The Fund in 1987, I had planned to leave after seven or eight years. I believed that new ideas and new perspectives were always needed after about that length of time, especially in organizations in which a founder is also the executive. In my experience in the nonprofit world, I had known too many founders who had stayed on too long. They became boring and bored — and the organization suffered by becoming stagnant. It is important for new people with different ideas to come in. That was my belief. Other people that I spoke with held that ten years should be the minimum stay for a founding executive.

Feeling the need to assess not only the situation of the organization but also my own part in it, in early 1995 I took three weeks off and went to New Zealand, where I spent time in solitude by the sea. Given the pressure of work and the dynamic growth of The Fund, it seemed impossible to take more time, though no doubt that would have been useful. I have always found that being alone in nature reveals wise answers to questions or dilemmas. I returned to California with the clear idea that I would leave The Global Fund within the next few months and certainly by the end of 1995. This was a period of change for me; my mother had died a few months before, and I was turning sixty in June. It seemed time to move on.

Searching for a New Staff Leader

At the June board meeting in 1995, I shared my decision to retire by the end of the year. I hoped that we would have a new person in place by the very beginning of 1996. People were surprised by and not particularly happy with my decision. Some were amazed that I would retire after nine hard and intense years spent bringing the organization to a state of health and renown. Others wondered why I would dare to leave such a successful, respected organization to face the unknown. Some board members, I learned later, felt abandoned. They told me that it was as if their mother had suddenly decided to leave them. Friends and colleagues presented various suggestions based on the classic models of organization: "Stay on." "Be chair of the board or president without the tasks of running the day-to-day organization." "Get an executive director who does the daily work." "Stay on and continue being the visionary." Such options did not appeal to me; they didn't fit my concept of a dynamic organization and the way in which such an organization should move into the future.

At the time I announced my plan to retire, I felt that The Global Fund was in place: the staff was capable; the programs and systems were clearly defined and stable; we had ongoing, significant funding; and our network was continuing to grow worldwide. I knew that the funding base, the operating systems, and the structures of the organization were solid enough for me to step aside and for the organization to continue in a healthy way.

"Not in [her] goals but in [her] transitions [wo]man is great." So said Emerson, slightly amended by me. I used this as a personal mantra throughout the transitional months that followed, months that proved unexpectedly painful. During those months, the search for my successor thoroughly challenged my faith that an organization could live by its principles. Although the outcome turned out to be positive, the process violated many of the principles that I thought we had held dear; it was carried out in a way that went against the style of The Global Fund to such an extent that it shocked me. I describe this experience to help you anticipate and possibly prevent such events in your transitions.

After we all returned from Beijing, the board turned to the task of finding my successor, and at the October 1995 meeting the board created a search committee of four board members and one staff representative. I felt strongly that we were moving to a new era and that this committee needed to be free of the influence of the founding president, so I noted early on that I would not serve as a member. The board members from outside of the United States were surprised and disappointed; American board members agreed with me, believing that I should not participate on the committee. We all agreed that I would be involved in the search process by providing names of possible candidates and by interviewing the final candidates.

The committee began its work by interviewing and selecting a consultant, an energetic woman working in a small search firm in California. Although this firm had done little with nonprofits and virtually nothing in the international field, the consultant had been recommended, she was enthusiastic about The Global Fund, and she impressed the committee. She began gathering names from Global Fund board members and other people connected with The Fund in the United States. But she decided, and the committee members agreed, that there would be no public announcement of this job opportunity, nor would there be a call for applications or unsolicited letters expressing interest. There would be no notification to our grantees and our international advisors that a search was in process; the search would not include a worldwide mailing to the members of The Global Fund network. It was decided that the process would be proactive, as in most U.S. corporate searches, rather than responsive to inquiries from individual people. Committee members and some others, including myself, would provide names of possible contacts, and the consultant would contact selected people who would in turn give us the names of people they thought should be contacted or would be possible candidates. In this way, many leads would come to the consultant's attention.

The reason for this closed approach was that the consultant feared that if our worldwide network were to be informed of this job opportunity The Global Fund would be inundated with unsolicited letters and overwhelmed with applications from people all around the world. I was not concerned about that because I trusted that interested women who would apply would be thoughtful about themselves and about what would be required to run an international organization.

I tried to hold back from expressing my extreme dismay at this exclusive approach. It went against The Global Fund principles of inclusiveness, responsiveness, transparency, and open communication, all of which had been hallmarks of the style of The Global Fund. It also bypassed our huge grantee and advisor network. After some discussion, the search committee and consultant agreed only that I would be permitted to write to our ninety-four advisors around the world informing them that a formal search had begun. At one meeting, the consultant told the staff that they were to say nothing to anyone about the search; they were to refer all callers who asked about the transition at The Global Fund to her, without any discussion, never mind that the person on the end of the phone line might be calling from some remote part of the world or speaking in a language other than English. This edict I reversed, probably confirming the belief that "founders cannot let go of organizations." But to me, it was simply unthinkable that our staff would close off discussions with women calling from far off places inquiring about the transition at The Fund.

I spoke with Dame Nita Barrow, who was the co-chair of the search committee, about my concerns, and she said that she saw little reason for a search firm or consultant at all. "The Global Fund has a fantastic international network," she told me. "We should surely select someone from within those networks." But the approach of Dame Nita was not to be; she died in December 1995 and was not replaced on the committee, thereby throwing off the hoped-for balance of a committee to be made up equally of U.S.- and non-U.S.-based members. I discussed this with the board chair, luchie pavia ticzon, and the committee drew in two non-U.S.-based members for the final interviews.

The search process went on, without public announcements or any mechanism that would allow feedback from our world-wide network. Only those whose names appeared on our lists would provide input, and that input was handled exclusively by the consultant, who did all of the preliminary interviewing. She became the funnel through which all information flowed: she made the telephone calls, she made judgments about the appropriateness of candidates, she narrowed down the lists, and she reported back to the committee. She did her job well, but this individualistic and closed style was so unlike anything The Global Fund had done before and, in fact, had stood for, that it amazed me. Several of us had worked so hard to make The Global Fund and its work truly global and transparent. In a few short months, the search process demonstrated that The Fund was a U.S. organization, based in the United States and operating within that culture.

Naturally, parts of the search process had to be kept confidential — such as the names of candidates — but as the process went on, it became more and more secret. I found it particularly difficult during that period to meet advisors and grantees at various conferences and to have to respond to questions and comments about the search. Time and again I heard such comments and questions as "I gather The Global Fund search is closed, Anne? I've heard nothing about it." Or, "Is there a job description publicly available? I'd love to see it." Or, "I was really surprised that the search had begun, Anne. I thought that we would be informed." Or, "Did The Global Fund think of hiring a non-U.S. firm or consultant?" These exchanges put me in the odd position of feeling I had to apologize for The Global Fund, something I had never had to do before. I found myself saying things like, "I think that the committee really is trying to be in touch with lots of people. My sense is that the consultant is speaking with many people." More direct questions about how "global" The Global Fund really was with such a search process, and whether we had abandoned our open ways and our learning style were even harder to respond to without sounding critical of the organization itself.

As it turned out, not one of the final six candidates had been part of our network of advisors, board members, grantees, or volunteers (although a couple of them became donors during the time of the search). The final candidates all came out of high-dollar donor institutions based in the United States, possibly an advantage but somewhat limited in concept. There were excellent candidates among the finalists, one of whom was chosen to be the next staff leader, so one might claim that the end justified the means. The outcome was good, but the process violated many principles of The Global Fund. That not one of the final candidates had emerged from the vast non-U.S.-based Global Fund network seemed odd, somehow not right. We had worked hard over the years at The Fund to be inclusive in a global sense, and suddenly The Global Fund was not.

My intentions in raising questions about the search process were questioned. I was concerned with principles, and I tried to make that clear. But some thought that I was not able to "let go" or that I was trying to undermine the process. It was true that I could not let go of the principles that had characterized The Global Fund, and I wished that the process had lived up to them. But my heart and mind had gone into the organization, and I only wished for its continued health.

I have since spoken to other founding executives of non-profits and corporations and have received some clarity. Most said that they had faced similar situations. Even though they themselves had set in motion the process of change and had worked diligently to make the transition graceful and successful, questions still arose about their intentions during the time of transition. There seems to be a stereotype of founders — that they cannot let go — even when it is the founder who wants to move on and make way for new leadership. This stereotype is sometimes reinforced by experience, but like all stereotypes, it is destructive and burdensome.

My advice to retiring founders and chief executives who wish to make a transition as smooth as possible is to walk away with little or no expectation of return for what you have put into the organization or how you have worked to develop a transition process that will be smooth. The most graceful transitions work because the founder or chief executive walks out of the garden and only reenters at the specific invitation of the new executive. The transition at The Global Fund was a good one by anyone's measure and certainly to the outside world. Although my successor invited me to feel free to come to The Global Fund whenever I wished and to visit anytime, I believed that the wise course was to visit only when invited on specific occasions. I think this conscious departure is essential to a graceful transition, odd as it sometimes may seem. My job in the final months of my tenure was to run the organization well; carry out the transition plan that I had laid out; secure stable and long-term funding; and welcome Kavita Ramdas, the new staff leader, whose commitment, intelligence, and enthusiasm were palpable and continue to be.

Moving Forward

It was important to me to complete the transition in leadership with a sense of excitement, of looking forward to new beginnings. I wanted to acknowledge and honor the new member joining the team of gardeners at The Global Fund. Along with her enthusiasm and commitment, Kavita also brought relevant experience to the next phase of The Global Fund's work. I especially liked it that Kavita was about my daughter's age; I thought it wonderful that we were consciously turning to the next generation. I also wanted to honor the older gardener (me!), who was moving to the edge, to cultivate new ground and nurture some other interesting and fragile plants. We tried to do all of this through a series of events, including a daylong retreat, that gave opportunities for celebration and reflection. Meanwhile, Kavita and I developed an understanding about how we would communicate and transmit important experience and information, much like the pact that Iuchie and I had developed.

Most of all, I wanted to believe that the work that we had chosen at The Global Fund — to transform the world through empowering women and women's groups — would continue, with unlimited and new possibilities ahead. I was pleased to be leaving the organization in an extremely healthy situation structurally, financially, and programmatically. By the time I left The Global Fund, we had a network of more than eight hundred groups, an Advisory Council of almost one hundred, and thousands of donors. We had given away more than one thousand grants totaling six million dollars in more than one hundred countries. We had a million dollars in the Reserve Fund — double my original goal, which was to have at least half a million dollars by the time I left The Global Fund. And we had already raised a hefty percentage of the next two years' budgets. Our databases were among the best in the world of philanthropy and certainly the most complete in the world of women's organizations. Our grant-making system was nonbureaucratic and efficient, a model of flexibility, simplicity, and accountability.

We had been as generous as we could be and had done our work flexibly, with respect and trust. We had been hardworking and devoted to our style of practicing our principles. We did what we said we would do and surpassed my original goal of giving away ten million dollars by the year 2000. (I was gone from The Global Fund by that time, but The Fund went significantly beyond that figure by the turn of the century and has continued to thrive.) Most of all, we had learned from hundreds of women as they shared with us their visions, their analyses of the state of the world, and their ingenious approaches to addressing extremely difficult issues. I left The Global Fund with the feeling that I had wrapped it all up in a lovely box with a big red ribbon and passed the whole thing on as a gift to those who were to follow.

I have been described as an unrealistic idealist. Well, yes. Was I proud of what we had accomplished during my years with The Global Fund? Yes, in a way. But my feelings were much more of wonderment and excitement.[1] The Global Fund had gone far beyond me and other individual people. It had become part of a way of thinking in the world that held that we could create a better world, that we could be good to one another, and that we could value each other and our planet. I had known intuitively that such a movement was both necessary and inevitable at this stage in the history of the world. I have been excited to be part of it and to be able to contribute to the lives of others around the world.

When I retired, I received many letters from women's groups overseas. These women reminded me that what we had been able to do in offering grants through The Global Fund was important, but that the way we carried out the work was even more important. Again and again I read, "It wasn't the money, it was the feeling that you were with us.... We knew that you were one of us, that we were connected, and that made all the difference." One letter stated simply, "You were us." That, I felt, was success.

A letter that particularly touched me came from Unity Dow and the staff and board of the Metlhaetsile Women's Information Centre in Botswana:

> Sitting here in Botswana, a semi desert, looking through the window and hoping for rain, I cannot think of a better farewell salute, than the traditional, "go with rain."
>
> We at Metlhaetsile [which means "the time has come"] wish you all the best, hope you will not move far away. We will always remember that The Global Fund For Women was the first donor to believe in us and trusted us enough to give us funds when all we had was a dream. After that, it became easier to convince other donors that we meant business. We thank you for this trust.
>
> If you are ever in this part of the world, look us up and we will be more than happy to introduce you to our patch of this global garden you have helped nurture.[2]

Now I was facing the classic dilemma that E. B. White had described: "Every morning I awake torn between a desire to save the world and an inclination to savor it. This makes it hard to plan the day."[3] I began to think about my new hopes and dreams.

What was next for me? I knew that I wanted to spend more time walking on beaches, being there for my family and friends, and playing and listening to music. I was leaving because we had realized my vision for an international network of women helping women; because I was tired of working so hard and dealing every day with tragic human rights issues; and certainly because I wanted to do some other things in my life.

Dear friends reminded me that about every ten years, I reconstitute my life. I decide to move on to something new, try another job, take up a new interest, acquire more space for my garden and my beehives. I was at such a transition point. In order to move forward, I knew that I needed to see the world anew. I was about to do just that.

Things to Remember
as You Cultivate Your Dreams

- Recognize clues that suggest it is time to make a change.

- Take time to rest, to recover, to listen to your heart.

- Consider the best interests of the whole and move to the edges consciously.

- Leave your program or organization in the best possible shape and pass it on as a gift.

- "Asked upon his retirement what his proudest moment was, Mr. [David] Packard responded instead with some plain-spoken advice on how to succeed: 'Do something useful, then forget about it and go on to the next thing.'"4 Sounds like good advice to me.

- As you consider whether to save the world or savor it, do both.

Epilogue

As I look to the future now, in my 70s, I realize that my perspective — but not my vision for the world — has changed from earlier times in my life. Now I find myself thinking in terms of how the future will affect other people, most personally, my grandchildren, and what those people will do to cope with change and opportunity.

I feel that in this, the third stage of life, I am at the edge of the garden, sharing, coaching, and continuing to learn. I feel very much that I have an important role in social change, but it is now from a different place. For me, that place has involved teaching undergraduate students at Stanford University, a wonderful way to learn from young people and share my experiences.

I continue to believe that we are in a time when the old regime — the old ways of doing things, with some people dominating others — is on the way out. I continue to see the current

violence in the world as the dinosaur flailing away as it disap-
pears from the earth. The students give me hope for the world;
they are so smart and articulate, so eager and hopeful.

My response to that Stanford student who called out for direction and advice after 9/11 was, in essence, that we are able to
add to the peace and beauty of the earth through kind and creative acts. I do not mean to beg the question of dealing with
evil, or to belittle the genuine dilemma of people who have
come to a point when anger, desperation, or hatred overwhelms
them and they can think of no way to approach life except
through acts of violence. I believe that we are in a time of violence — and yet I have hope, and I know there are things that
each of us can do.

Since leaving The Global Fund, among other ways of savor-
ing the world, I have spent more time in my garden, and that has
enabled me to see the world anew. New plants grow from piles
of dead leaves. Occasionally a noxious weed enters and needs to
be removed. An insect or a bird flies through and fertilizes a
flower or drops a seed. There is always something new to observe, to hear, to smell, or to learn in a garden. It is the place
where beginnings and endings, cosmic visions and tiny miracles
are found. Just as I conceived of The Global Fund as a kind of
wild garden, I see the garden as a microcosm of the world. And
in my garden, I can always imagine and experience peace.

Things to Do
to Cultivate the Global Garden

We *can* take actions that will affect the quality of our lives and
the quality of the relationships that we have with others. We *can*
do our parts to change the world in powerful ways. We can each

look within ourselves, understand our uniqueness and our strengths. And then, feeling secure within ourselves, we can and must take risks by doing these kinds of things:

- Dream of positive change and know that, working in concert with others, you can make a difference.

- Speak out with your own unique voice when you observe inequality.

- Speak with men about violence against women.

- Protest violence and war — they are not acceptable strategies.

- Write to your governmental representatives so that they do not feel isolated and can more truly represent your views.

- Teach your sons and daughters to value each other, deeply, and to respect their equality and their differences.

- Give money and time to organizations that are doing good.

- Speak out whenever you observe injustice, whenever people of difference are being demeaned, or when negative stereotypes are being reinforced.

- Act powerfully in the context of love and compassion, respecting the cycles of the earth and expressing a love and concern for the generations that follow.

- Embrace diversity and eliminate the concept of "the other."

- Recognize your own power and constantly share it.

- If in doubt, say yes.

- If in doubt, be generous and giving.

- If in doubt, choose compassion over anger — anger is disempowering.

- Choose integration over fragmentation.

- Be efficient and effective in your work, and still treat others softly.

- Decide what you want to do, focus, and do your work with excellence.

- Be willing to be vulnerable — which is not about weakness but about truth.

- Find strength through positive connection with others.

- Value freedom and know that it emerges from trust and love.

<hr/>

As more and more of us take these kinds of steps toward a shared vision, the qualities of compassion and connection will increasingly become the norms in society as a whole. We will then be able to change our paradigm of social interaction from *either/or* to *both/and*, from *win/lose* to *win/win*. To manage diversity, to create organizations and communities that truly include and go further to exchange and share, to interact with learning and love — these are the challenges of our time. Meeting them will give meaning to our lives. So much depends upon how we choose to treat one another.

Gratitudes

———— ⬿⬿⬿⬿ ————

Many people have helped, inspired, cajoled, and pushed me as I put together this book, and some have been particularly helpful and persistent. I especially thank Esther Hewlett for her unwavering support over the years and for her insistence that I finish this project. Esther's and my coffee meetings have been nurturing and memorable. I thank Barb Waugh both for insisting that I get back on track with this book and also for working with Laurie Mittelstadt to include me as one of the one thousand women nominated for the Nobel Peace Prize in 2005. Barbara's efforts were key to my returning to work on the book.

Starting a few years ago, Chris Harris of the Ford Foundation, Rita Thapa of Tewa (which means "support"), an organization that assists women's efforts in Nepal, and Hope Chigudu of the Zimbabwe Women's Resource Centre and Network urged me to write about founding and developing The Global Fund for Women. This book is not strictly about that, but it is a beginning. I thank them for suggesting that I pull my thoughts together.

A month in 1996 at a blissful women's writing center, Hedge-brook, on Whidbey Island in Washington State, laid the ground-work for this book. Elan Garonzik of the Charles Stewart Mott Foundation and Mark Rosenman of The Union Institute also made it possible for me to have some free time to think about this and other writing projects. Holly Gibson provided early ed-itorial help, and, more recently, Yvette Bozzini worked with me to make the book happen. Katherine Martin led me to New World Library, where Georgia Hughes and Kristen Cashman helped me so much. I thank them all sincerely.

With regard to the creation of The Global Fund for Women, I could name and thank hundreds of people who made a differ-ence to me and who were there for me in the early years. They were among the grantees, advisors, board members, staff, and donors. They are too numerous to list, but they were my not-so-silent partners in creating and developing The Fund between 1987 and 1996. When the early history of The Fund is written, they will be acknowledged appropriately.

Loving thanks go to my daughter, Gwyn Firth Murray, for her clear advice and confidence when I hesitated to take on the job of creating The Global Fund. Finally, I thank my friend Barry Rose for many wise contributions, not the least of which was the idea for the title of this book. He and I greatly value freedom, and we know that it emerges from trust and love.

Notes

Book epigraph: This statement seems to have been derived
from a quotation from Mohandas Karamchand "Mahatma"
Gandhi, the "father" of the independence of India from
British colonial rule: "Find purpose, the means will follow."

Prologue

Epigraph: Bessie Stanley, *Lincoln Sentinel* (November 30, 1905).
A different version is sometimes attributed to Ralph Waldo
Emerson.

1. The Global Fund for Women, *The First Two Years,*
1987–1989.
2. Peter M. Senge, *The Fifth Discipline: The Art and Practice of*
the Learning Organization (New York: Doubleday/Currency,
1990).
3. Thich Nhat Hanh, *True Love: A Practice for Awakening the*
Heart (Boston: Shambhala, 2004), p. 9.

4. Vaclav Havel, "The Need for Transcendence in the Postmodern World," a speech delivered in Independence Hall in Philadelphia, Pennsylvania (July 4, 1994), when Havel was awarded the Philadelphia Liberty Medal.

Chapter 1: Believe Positive Change Is Possible

Epigraph: Tony Kushner, quoted by David Brooks in "The Fog of Peace," *The Weekly Standard*, September 30, 2002.

1. *The Day After*, directed by Nicholas Meyer (aired by ABC, November 20, 1983).

2. Jonathan Schell, *The Fate of the Earth* (New York: Knopf, 1982).

3. Carol Gilligan, *In a Different Voice: Psychological Theory and Women's Development* (Cambridge, MA: Harvard University Press, 1982).

4. Edward C. Whitmont, *The Return of the Goddess* (New York: Crossroad, 1982).

5. Albert Einstein, quoted in Margaret Wheatley, *Leadership and the New Science* (San Francisco: Berrett-Koehler, 1992).

6. This quote is often attributed to Martin Niemöller, a Nazi-era pastor of the Lutheran Church in Dahlem, a wealthy suburb of Berlin, who opposed Hitler's policies and who said this by way of confession when the allies liberated the concentration camp where he spent World War II. The quote is discussed by Franklin H. Littell in *Christian Ethics Today*, February 1997.

7. United Nations Development Programme, *Human Development Report, 1995*.

8. Celia W. Dugger, "U.N. Reports Lack of Data on Women in Poverty," *New York Times*, January 21, 2006. Dugger's article reported on the United Nations publication *The World's Women, 2005: Progress in Statistics*.

9. Elise Boulding, in a personal communication to the author, fall 1987.

10. Whitmont, *The Return of the Goddess*, p. vii, quoted in The Global Fund for Women, *The First Two Years, 1987-1989*, p. 3.

Chapter 2: Be True to Yourself and Learn

Epigraph: Martha Graham, in a letter to Agnes de Mille, quoted in de Mille's book *Martha: The Life and Work of Martha Graham* (New York: Random House, 1991).

1. Betty Friedan, *The Feminine Mystique* (New York: Norton, 1963).

2. André Gide, *The Counterfeiters: A Novel* (New York: Vintage, 1973), p. 353.

3. Henry David Thoreau, *Walden and "Civil Disobedience"* (New York: Signet, 1999), p. 275.

4. Thich Nhat Hanh, *True Love: A Practice for Awakening the Heart* (Boston: Shambhala, 2004), p. 9.

5. T. H. White, *The Once and Future King* (New York: Ace Books, 1987), quoted in Parker J. Palmer, *The Courage to Teach* (San Francisco: Jossey-Bass, 1998), p.141.

6. James Stephens, *The Crock of Gold* (New York: Collier Books, 1912), pp. 128ff.

Chapter 3: Connect to Build Trust and Freedom

Epigraph: Margaret Mead, used by courtesy of the Institute for Intercultural Studies, Inc., New York.

1. E. M. Forster, *Howard's End* (New York: Vintage International Edition, 1989), p. 195.

2. Thich Nhat Hanh, *True Love: A Practice for Awakening the Heart* (Boston: Shambhala, 2004), p. 9.

Chapter 4: Dream and Clarify Your Vision

Epigraph: From an Easter sermon delivered in 1998 at St. Mark's Episcopal Church in Palo Alto, California.

1. Joshua Cooper Ramo, "How AOL Lost the Battle but Won the War," *Time* (September 22, 1997).
2. Paul Hawken, *Growing a Business* (New York: Fireside, 1988).
3. Pam Muñoz Ryan, *Riding Freedom* (New York: Scholastic, 1998), p. 1.
4. Martha Graham, in a letter to Agnes de Mille, quoted in de Mille's book *Martha: The Life and Work of Martha Graham* (New York: Random House, 1991).
5. Helen Adams Keller, *The Open Door* (Garden City, NY: Doubleday, 1957).

Chapter 5: Practice Your Principles to Avoid Confusion

Epigraph: Kurt Vonnegut, Jr., *The Sirens of Titan* (New York: Delacorte, 1959).

1. David Packard, *The HP Way: How Bill Hewlett and I Built Our Business* (New York: HarperBusiness, 1995).
2. William Strunk, Jr., and E. B. White, *The Elements of Style* (New York: Macmillan Company), 1959.
3. Sir Arthur Quiller-Couch, *On the Art of Writing*, XII, "On Style, 1916" (Mineola, NY: Dover Publications, 2006).
4. Peter M. Senge, *The Fifth Discipline: The Art and Practice of the Learning Organization* (New York: Doubleday/ Currency, 1990).
5. The Global Fund for Women, in annual reports of the first nine years, donor listings.

Chapter 6: Grow Strong and Stay Lean

Epigraph: William R. Hewlett, cofounder of the Hewlett-
Packard Company, in conversation with the author,
September 1987.

1. A few years after I had that conversation with Bill Hewlett,
   I read Margaret Wheatley's *Leadership and the New Science*
   (San Francisco: Berrett-Koehler Publishers, 1992).
   Wheatley's ideas (on pp. 42ff) very much express not only
   what I had felt intuitively when I explained the vision to
   Bill Hewlett but also what turned out to be my experience
   with The Global Fund's support of many small groups
   worldwide. Wheatley wrote, "These changes in small
   places...create large-systems change, not because they
   build one upon the other, but because they share in the
   unbroken wholeness that has united them all along. Our
   activities in one part of the whole create non-local causes
   that emerge far from us. There is value in working with the
   system anyplace it manifests because unseen connections
   will create effects at a distance, in places we never thought.
   This model of change—of small starts, surprises, unseen
   connections, quantum leaps—matches our experience more
   closely than our favored models of incremental change."
2. Edward Abbey, quoted by Richard J. Douthwaite in *The
   Growth Illusion: How Economic Growth Has Enriched the
   Few, Impoverished the Many, and Endangered the Planet*
   (Tulsa, OK: Council Oak Books, 1993).
3. Lao Tzu, in Rau Grigg, *The New Lao Tzu: A Contemporary
   Tao Te Ching* (Boston: Tuttle, 1995), p. 52.
4. John W. Gardner, farewell speech upon retiring as founding
   chairperson of the Independent Sector, Washington DC, 1983.

Chapter 7: Govern, Manage, and Evaluate for Empowerment

Epigraph: This prayer was discovered on a 14th century soldier's gravestone in England. Another version, often attributed to Reinhold Niebuhr, is the following, which has been used as a "serenity" prayer by members of Alcoholics Anonymous: "God, give me the grace to accept the things I cannot change, the courage to change the things I can, and the wisdom to know the difference."

1. Antoine de Saint-Exupéry, *Wind, Sand, and Stars* (New York: Harcourt, 1992), p. 215.
2. Michele Andina, RN, PhD, and Barbara Pillsbury, PhD, *Trust: An Approach to Women's Empowerment* (Los Angeles: Pacific Institute for Women's Health, 1998).
3. Michael Scriven is a professor of evaluation at the University of Auckland in New Zealand and a professor of psychology at Claremont Graduate University in California.

Chapter 8: Be Generous and Raise Money

1. This statement seems to have been derived from a quotation from Mohandas Karamchand "Mahatma" Gandhi, the "father" of the independence of India from British colonial rule: "Find purpose, the means will follow."
2. Federal Bureau of Investigation, famous cases. See http://www.fbi.gov/libref/historic/famcases/sutton/sutton.htm (accessed February 2006).
3. Benjamin Franklin, *The Autobiography of Benjamin Franklin* (New York: Touchstone, 2004), p. 102.

Chapter 9: Lead and Share Leadership

1. Carol Gilligan, *In a Different Voice: Psychological Theory and Women's Development* (Cambridge, MA: Harvard University Press, 1982).

2. See http://www.awdf.org.
3. From a newsletter on leadership published by the
   Independent Sector (IS), Washington DC, 1992. IS had
   expanded its definition considerably by 1992. In 1986–88,
   the Independent Sector's Leadership Studies Program
   published a series of monographs by John Gardner on the
   nature of leadership, in which he used this definition:
   "Leadership... is the process of persuasion and example by
   which an individual (or leadership team) induces a group
   to take action that is in accord with the leader's purposes
   or the shared purposes of all."

Chapter 10: Plan and Know When to Move On

Epigraph: Author, amending a quote by Ralph Waldo Emerson,
The Complete Works of Ralph Waldo Emerson, vol. 12, Natural
History of the Intellect (Cambridge: Riverside, 1903–04).
1. Although Margaret Wheatley uses a music metaphor in
   describing leadership, her words describe my feelings "in
   the end": "As leaders we play a crucial role in selecting the
   melody, setting the tempo, establishing the key, and inviting
   the players. But... the music comes from something we
   cannot direct, from a unified whole created among the
   players — a relational holism that transcends separateness.
   In the end, when it works, we sit back, amazed and
   grateful." Margaret Wheatley, *Leadership and the New
   Science* (San Francisco: Berrett-Koehler, 1992), p. 44.
2. Unity Dow and staff of Metlhaetsile Women's Information
   Centre, letter to author, October 1996.
3. E. B. White, quoted in Israel Shenker, "E. B. White: Notes
   and Comment by Author," *New York Times*, July 11, 1969.
4. David Packard, quoted in his obituary by Lawrence M.
   Fisher in *The New York Times*, March 27, 1996.

Index

∽∽∼◦∼∽∽

About the Author

Anne Firth Murray, a New Zealander, attended the University of California, Berkeley, and New York University, where she studied economics, political science, and public administration, with a focus on international health policy and women's reproductive health. She has worked at the United Nations as a writer, has taught in Hong Kong and Singapore, and has spent several years as an editor with Oxford, Stanford, and Yale University presses.

For the past twenty-five years, she has worked in the field of philanthropy, serving as a consultant to many foundations. From 1978 to the end of 1987, she directed the environment and international population programs of the William and Flora Hewlett Foundation in California. She is the founding president of The Global Fund for Women, established in 1987, which provides funds internationally to seed, strengthen, and link groups committed to women's well-being. She is currently a consulting professor in the human biology program at Stanford University.

Ms. Murray has served on numerous boards and councils of nonprofit organizations, currently including the African Women's Development Fund, Commonweal, GRACE (a group working on HIV/AIDS in east Africa), the Hesperian Foundation, and UNNITI (a women's foundation in India). She is the recipient of many awards and honors for her work on women's health and philanthropy, and in 2005 she was among one thousand women nominated for the Nobel Peace Prize. Ms. Murray has one daughter, who is an attorney in California, and two grandchildren. She lives in Menlo Park, California.

To learn more, please visit www.paradigmfound.org.